The Valley of Democracy

Meredith Nicholson

Alpha Editions

This edition published in 2024

ISBN : 9789362095411

Design and Setting By
Alpha Editions
www.alphaedis.com
Email - info@alphaedis.com

As per information held with us this book is in Public Domain.
This book is a reproduction of an important historical work. Alpha Editions uses the best technology to reproduce historical work in the same manner it was first published to preserve its original nature. Any marks or number seen are left intentionally to preserve its true form.

Contents

THE VALLEY OF DEMOCRACY .... - 1 -
CHAPTER I THE FOLKS AND THEIR FOLKSINESS ...... - 2 -
CHAPTER II TYPES AND DIVERSIONS .... - 20 -
CHAPTER III THE FARMER OF THE MIDDLE WEST .. - 42 -
CHAPTER IV CHICAGO .... - 67 -
CHAPTER V THE MIDDLE WEST IN POLITICS .... - 89 -
CHAPTER VI THE SPIRIT OF THE WEST .... - 114 -
FOOTNOTES: .... - 136 -

THE VALLEY OF DEMOCRACY

France evoked from the unknown the valley that may, in more than one sense, be called the heart of America.... The chief significance and import of the addition of this valley to the maps of the world, all indeed that makes it significant, is that here was given (though not of deliberate intent) a rich, wide, untouched field, distant, accessible only to the hardiest, without a shadowing tradition or a restraining fence, in which men of all races were to make attempt to live together under rules of their own devising and enforcing. And as here the government of the people by the people was to have even more literal interpretation than in that Atlantic strip which had traditions of property suffrage and church privilege and class distinctions, I have called it the "Valley of the New Democracy."

—JOHN H. FINLEY: "The French in the Heart of America."

CHAPTER I
THE FOLKS AND THEIR FOLKSINESS

I

"THE great trouble with these fellows down here," remarked my friend as we left the office of a New York banker—"the trouble with all of 'em is that they forget about the *Folks*. You noticed that when he asked in his large, patronizing way how things are going out West he didn't wait for us to answer; he pressed a button and told his secretary to bring in those tables of railroad earnings and to-day's crop bulletins and that sort of rubbish, so he could tell *us*. It never occurs to 'em that the Folks are human beings and not just a column of statistics. Why, the *Folks*——"

My friend, an orator of distinction, formerly represented a tall-corn district in Congress. He drew me into Trinity churchyard and discoursed in a vein with which I had long been familiar upon a certain condescension in Easterners, and the East's intolerable ignorance of the ways and manners, the hopes and aims, of the West, which move him to rage and despair. I was aware that he was gratified to have an opportunity to unbosom himself at the brazen gates of Wall Street, and equally conscious that he was experimenting upon me with phrases that he was coining for use on the hustings. They were so used, not without effect, in the campaign of 1916—a contest whose results were well calculated to draw attention to the "Folks" as an upstanding, independent body of citizens.

Folks is recognized by the lexicographers as an American colloquialism, a variant of folk. And folk, in old times, was used to signify the commonalty, the plain people. But my friend, as he rolled "Folks" under his tongue there in the shadow of Trinity, used it in a sense that excluded the hurrying midday Broadway throng and restricted its application to an infinitely superior breed of humanity, to be found on farms, in villages and cities remote from tidewater. His passion for democracy, his devotion to the commonweal, is not wasted upon New Englanders or Middle States people. In the South there are Folks, yes; his own people had come out of North Carolina, lingered a while in Kentucky, and lodged finally in Indiana, whence, following a common law of dispersion, they sought new homes in Illinois and Kansas. Beyond the Rockies there are Folks; he meets their leaders in national conventions; but they are only second cousins of those valiant freemen who rallied to the call of Lincoln and followed Grant and Sherman into battles that shook the continent. My friend's point of view is held by great numbers of people in that region we now call the Middle West. This attitude or state of mind with regard to the East is not to be taken too seriously; it is a part of the national humor, and has been expressed with delightful vivacity and candor in Mr. William Allen White's refreshing essay, "Emporia and New York."

A definition of Folks as used all the way from Ohio to Colorado, and with particular point and pith by the haughty sons and daughters of Indiana and Kansas, may be set down thus:

FOLKS. *n.* A superior people, derived largely from the Anglo-Saxon and Celtic races and domiciled in those northern States of the American Union whose waters fall into the Mississippi. Their *folksiness* (*q. v.*) is expressed in sturdy independence, hostility to capitalistic influence, and a proneness to social and political experiment. They are strong in the fundamental virtues, more or less sincerely averse to conventionality, and believe themselves possessed of a breadth of vision and a devotion to the common good at once beneficent and unique in the annals of mankind.

We of the West do not believe—not really—that we are the only true interpreters of the dream of democracy. It pleases us to swagger a little when we speak of ourselves as the Folks and hint at the dire punishments we hold in store for monopoly and privilege; but we are far less dangerous than an outsider, bewildered or annoyed by our apparent bitterness, may be led to believe. In our hearts we do not think ourselves the only good Americans. We merely feel that the East began patronizing us and that anything we may do in that line has been forced upon us by years of outrageous contumely. And when New York went to bed on the night of election day, 1916, confident that as went the Empire State so went the Union, it was only that we of the West might chortle the next morning to find that Ah Sin had forty packs concealed in his sleeve and spread them out on the Sierra Nevadas with an air that was child-like and bland.

Under all its jauntiness and cocksureness, the West is extremely sensitive to criticism. It likes admiration, and expects the Eastern visitor to be properly impressed by its achievements, its prodigious energy, its interpretation and practical application of democracy, and the earnestness with which it interests itself in the things of the spirit. Above all else it does not like to appear absurd. According to its light it intends to do the right thing, but it yields to laughter much more quickly than abuse if the means to that end are challenged.

The pioneers of the older States endured hardships quite as great as the Middle Westerners; they have contributed as generously to the national life in war and peace; the East's aid to the West, in innumerable ways, is immeasurable. I am not thinking of farm mortgages, but of nobler things— of men and women who carried ideals of life and conduct, of justice and law, into new territory where such matters were often lightly valued. The prowler in these Western States recognizes constantly the trail of New Englanders who founded towns, built schools, colleges, and churches, and left an ineffaceable stamp upon communities. Many of us Westerners sincerely admire the East and do reverence to Eastern gods when we can sneak unobserved into the temples. We dispose of our crops and merchandise as quickly as possible, that we may be seen of men in New York. Western school-teachers pour into New England every summer on pious pilgrimages to Concord and Lexington. And yet we feel ourselves, the great body of us, a peculiar people. "Ten days of New York, and it's me for my home town" in Ohio, Indiana, Kansas, or Colorado. This expresses a very general feeling in the provinces.

It is far from my purpose to make out a case for the West as the true home of the Folks in these newer connotations of that noun, but rather to record some of the phenomena observable in those commonwealths where we are assured the Folks maintain the only true ark of the covenant of democracy. Certain concessions may be assumed in the unconvinced spectator whose path lies in less-favored portions of the nation. The West does indubitably coax an enormous treasure out of its soil to be tossed into the national hopper, and it does exert a profound influence upon the national life; but its manner of thought is different: it arrives at conclusions by processes that strike the Eastern mind as illogical and often as absurd or dangerous. The two great mountain ranges are barriers that shut it in a good deal by itself in spite of every facility of communication; it is disposed to be scornful of the world's experience where the experience is not a part of its own history. It believes that forty years of Illinois or Wisconsin are better than a cycle of Cathay, and it is prepared to prove it.

"Ten days of New York, and it's me for my home town."

The West's philosophy is a compound of Franklin and Emerson, with a dash of Whitman. Even Washington is a pale figure behind the Lincoln of its own prairies. Its curiosity is insatiable; its mind is speculative; it has a supreme confidence that upon an agreed state of facts the Folks, sitting as a high court, will hand down to the nation a true and just decision upon any matter in controversy. It is a patient listener. Seemingly tolerant of false prophets, it amiably gives them hearing in thousands of forums while awaiting an opportunity to smother their ambitions on election day. It will not, if it knows itself, do anything supremely foolish. Flirting with Greenbackism and Free Silver, it encourages the assiduous wooers shamelessly and then calmly sends them about their business. Maine can approach her election booths as coyly as Ohio or Nebraska, and yet the younger States rejoice in the knowledge that after all nothing is decided until they have been heard from. Politics becomes, therefore, not merely a matter for concern when some great contest is forward, but the year round it crowds business hard for first place in public affection.

II

The people of the Valley of Democracy (I am indebted for this phrase to Dr. John H. Finley) do a great deal of thinking and talking; they brood over the world's affairs with a peculiar intensity; and, beyond question, they exchange opinions with a greater freedom than their fellow citizens in other parts of America. I have travelled between Boston and New York on many occasions and have covered most of New England in railway journeys without ever being addressed by a stranger; but seemingly in the West men travel merely to cultivate the art of conversation. The gentleman who borrows your newspaper returns it with a crisp comment on the day's events. He is from Beatrice, or Fort Collins, perhaps, and you quickly find that he lives next door to the only man you know in his home town. You praise Nebraska, and he meets you in a generous spirit of reciprocity and compliments Iowa, Minnesota, or any other commonwealth you may honor with your citizenship.

The West is proud of its talkers, and is at pains to produce them for the edification of the visitor. In Kansas a little while ago my host summoned a friend of his from a town eighty miles away that I might hear him talk. And it was well worth my while to hear that gentleman talk; he is the best talker I have ever heard. He described for me great numbers of politicians past and present, limning them with the merciless stroke of a skilled caricaturist, or, in a benignant mood, presented them in ineffaceable miniature. He knew Kansas as he knew his own front yard. It was a delight to listen to discourse so free, so graphic in its characterizations, so colored and flavored with the very soil. Without impropriety I may state that this gentleman is Mr. Henry J. Allen, of the Wichita *Beacon*; the friend who produced him for my instruction and entertainment is Mr. William Allen White of the Emporia *Gazette*. Since this meeting I have heard Mr. Allen talk on other occasions without any feeling that I should modify my estimate of his conversational powers. In his most satisfying narrative, "The Martial Adventures of Henry and Me," Mr. White has told how he and Mr. Allen, as agents of the Red Cross, bore the good news of the patriotism and sympathy of Kansas to England, France, and Italy, and certainly America could have sent no more heartening messengers to our allies.

I know of no Western town so small that it doesn't boast at least one wit or story-teller who is exhibited as a special mark of honor for the entertainment of guests. As often as not these stars are women, who discuss public matters with understanding and brilliancy. The old superstition that women are deficient in humor never struck me as applicable to American women anywhere; certainly it is not true of Western women. In a region where story-telling flourishes, I can match the best male anecdotalist with a woman who can evoke mirth by neater and defter means.

The Western State is not only a political but a social unit. It is like a club, where every one is presumably acquainted with every one else. The railroads and interurbans carry an enormous number of passengers who are solely upon pleasure bent. The observer is struck by the general sociability, the astonishing amount of visiting that is in progress. In smoking compartments and in day coaches any one who is at all folksy may hear talk that is likely to prove informing and stimulating. And this cheeriness and volubility of the people one meets greatly enhances the pleasure of travel. Here one is reminded constantly of the provincial confidence in the West's greatness and wisdom in every department of human endeavor.

In January of last year it was my privilege to share with seven other passengers the smoking-room of a train out of Denver for Kansas City. The conversation was opened by a vigorous, elderly gentleman who had, he casually remarked, crossed Kansas six times in a wagon. He was a native of Illinois, a graduate of Asbury (Depauw) College, Indiana, a Civil War veteran, and he had been a member of the Missouri Legislature. He lived on a ranch in Colorado, but owned a farm in Kansas and was hastening thither to test his acres for oil. The range of his adventures was amazing; his acquaintance embraced men of all sorts and conditions, including Buffalo Bill, whose funeral he had just attended in Denver. He had known General George A. Custer and gave us the true story of the massacre of that hero and his command on the Little Big Horn. He described the "bad men" of the old days, many of whom had honored him with their friendship. At least three of the company had enjoyed like experiences and verified or amplified his statements. This gentleman remarked with undisguised satisfaction that he had not been east of the Mississippi for thirty years!

I fancied that he acquired merit with all the trans-Mississippians present by this declaration. However, a young commercial traveller who had allowed it to become known that he lived in New York seemed surprised, if not pained, by the revelation. As we were passing from one dry State to another we fell naturally into a discussion of prohibition as a moral and economic factor. The drummer testified to its beneficent results in arid territory with which he was familiar; one effect had been increased orders from his Colorado customers. It was apparent that his hearers listened with approval; they were citizens of dry States and it tickled their sense of their own rectitude that a pilgrim from the remote East should speak favorably of their handiwork. But the young gentleman, warmed by the atmosphere of friendliness created by his remarks, was guilty of a grave error of judgment.

"It's all right for these Western towns," he said, "but you could never put it over in New York. New York will never stand for it. London, Paris, New York—there's only one New York!"

The deep sigh with which he concluded, expressive of the most intense loyalty, the most poignant homesickness, and perhaps a thirst of long accumulation, caused six cigars, firmly set in six pairs of jaws, to point disdainfully at the ceiling. No one spoke until the offender had betaken himself humbly to bed. The silence was eloquent of pity for one so abandoned. That any one privileged to range the cities of the West should, there at the edge of the great plain, set New York apart for adoration, was too impious, too monstrous, for verbal condemnation.

Young women seem everywhere to be in motion in the West, going home from schools, colleges, or the State universities for week-ends, or attending social functions in neighboring towns. Last fall I came down from Green Bay in a train that was becalmed for several hours at Manitowoc. I left the crowded day coach to explore that pleasing haven and, returning, found that my seat had been pre-empted by a very charming young person who was reading my magazine with the greatest absorption. We agreed that the seat offered ample space for two and that there was no reason in equity or morals why she should not finish the story she had begun. This done, she commented upon it frankly and soundly and proceeded to a brisk discussion of literature in general. Her range of reading had been wide—indeed, I was embarrassed by its extent and impressed by the shrewdness of her literary appraisements. She was bound for a normal school where she was receiving instruction, not for the purpose of entering into the pedagogical life immediately, but to obtain a teacher's license against a time when it might become necessary for her to earn a livelihood. Every girl, she believed, should fit herself for some employment.

Manifestly she was not a person to ask favors of destiny: at eighteen she had already made terms with life and tossed the contract upon the knees of the gods. The normal school did not require her presence until the day after to-morrow, and she was leaving the train at the end of an hour to visit a friend who had arranged a dance in her honor. If that species of entertainment interested me, she said, I might stop for the dance. Engagements farther down the line precluded the possibility of my accepting this invitation, which was extended with the utmost circumspection, as though she were offering an impersonal hospitality supported by the sovereign dignity of the commonwealth of Wisconsin. When the train slowed down at her station a commotion on the platform announced the presence of a reception committee of considerable magnitude, from which I inferred that her advent was an incident of importance to the community. As she bade me good-by she tore apart a bouquet of fall flowers she had been carrying, handed me half of them, and passed from my sight forever. My exalted opinion of the young women of Wisconsin was strengthened on another occasion by a chance meeting with two graduates of the State University who were my fellow voyagers on a steamer that bumped into a riotous hurricane on its way down Lake Michigan. On the slanting deck they discoursed of political economy with a zest and humor that greatly enlivened my respect for the dismal science.

The listener in the West accumulates data touching the tastes and ambitions of the people of which local guide-books offer no hint. A little while ago two ladies behind me in a Minneapolis street-car discussed Cardinal Newman's "Dream of Gerontius," with as much avidity as though it were the newest novel. Having found that the apostles of free verse had captured and fortified Denver and Omaha, it was a relief to encounter these Victorian pickets on the upper waters of the Mississippi.

III

One is struck by the remarkable individuality of the States, towns, and cities of the West. State boundaries are not merely a geographical expression: they mark real differences of opinion, habit, custom, and taste. This is not a sentimental idea; any one may prove it for himself by crossing from Illinois into Wisconsin, or from Iowa into Nebraska. Kansas and Nebraska, though cut out of the same piece, not only seem different but they *are* different. Interest in local differentiations, in shadings of the "color" derived from a common soil, keep the visitor alert. To be sure the Ladies of the Lakes—Chicago, Cleveland, Detroit, Milwaukee, Toledo, Duluth—have physical aspects in common, but the similarity ends there. The literature of chambers of commerce as to the number of freight-cars handled or increases of population are of no assistance in a search for the causes of diversities in aim, spirit, and achievement.

The alert young cities watch each other enviously—they are enormously proud and anxious not to be outbettered in the struggle for perfection. In many places one is conscious of an effective leadership, of a man or a group of men and women who plant a target and rally the citizenry to play for the bull's-eye. A conspicuous instance of successful individual leadership is offered by Kansas City, where Mr. William R. Nelson, backed by his admirable newspaper, *The Star*, fought to the end of his life to make his city a better place to live in. Mr. Nelson was a remarkably independent and courageous spirit, his journalistic ideals were the highest, and he was deeply concerned for the public welfare, not only in the more obvious sense, but equally in bringing within the common reach enlightening influences that are likely to be neglected in new communities. Kansas City not only profited by Mr. Nelson's wisdom and generosity in his lifetime, but the community will receive ultimately his entire fortune. I am precluded from citing in other cities men still living who are distinguished by a like devotion to public service, but

I have chosen Mr. Nelson as an eminent example of the force that may be wielded by a single citizen.

Minneapolis offers a happy refutation of a well-established notion that a second generation is prone to show a weakened fibre. The sons of the men who fashioned this vigorous city have intelligently and generously supported many undertakings of highest value. The Minneapolis art museum and school and an orchestra of widening reputation present eloquent testimony to the city's attitude toward those things that are more excellent. Contrary to the usual history, these were not won as the result of laborious effort but rose spontaneously. The public library of this city not only serves the hurried business man through a branch in the business district, equipped with industrial and commercial reference books, but keeps pace with the local development in art and music by assembling the best literature in these departments. Both Minneapolis and Kansas City are well advertised by their admirably managed, progressive libraries. More may be learned from a librarian as to the trend of thought in his community than from the secretary of a commercial body. It is significant that last year, when municipal affairs were much to the fore in Kansas City, there was a marked increase in the use of books on civic and kindred questions. The latest report of the librarian recites that "as the library more nearly meets the wants of the community, the proportion of fiction used grows less, being but 34 per cent of the whole issue for the year." Similar impulses and achievements are manifested in Cleveland, a city that has written many instructive chapters in the history of municipal government. Since her exposition of 1904 and the splendid pageant of 1914 crystallized public aspiration, St. Louis has experienced a new birth of civic pride. Throughout the West American art has found cordial support. In Cleveland, Toledo, Detroit, Cincinnati, Indianapolis, St. Louis, Chicago, Minneapolis, Omaha, and Kansas City there are noteworthy specimens of the best work of American painters. The art schools connected with the Western museums have exercised a salutary influence in encouraging local talent, not only in landscape and portraiture, but in industrial designing.

By friendly co-operation on the part of Chicago and St. Louis smaller cities are able to enjoy advantages that would otherwise be beyond their reach. Lectures, orchestras, and travelling art exhibits that formerly stopped at Chicago or jumped thence to California, now find a hearty welcome in Kansas City, Omaha, and Denver. Thus Indianapolis was among the few cities that shared a few years ago in the comprehensive presentation of Saint Gaudens's work. The expense of the undertaking was not inconsiderable, but merchants and manufacturers bought tickets for distribution among their employees and met the demand with a generosity that left a balance in the art association's treasury. These Western cities, with their political and social problems, their rough edges, smoke, and impudent intrusions of tracks and chimneys due to rapid development and phenomenal prosperity, present art literally as the handmaiden of industry—

"All-lovely Art, stern Labor's fair-haired child."

If any one thing is quite definitely settled throughout this territory it is that yesterday's leaves have been plucked from the calendar: this verily is the land of to-morrow. One does not stand beside the Missouri at Omaha and indulge long in meditations upon the turbulent history and waywardness of that tawny stream; the cattle receipts for the day may have broken all records, but there are schools that must be seen, a collection of pictures to visit, or lectures to attend. I unhesitatingly pronounce Omaha the lecture centre of the world—reception committees flutter at the arrival of all trains. Man does not live by bread alone—not even in the heart of the corn belt in a city that haughtily proclaims itself the largest primary butter-market in the world! It is the great concern of Kansas that it shall miss nothing; to cross that commonwealth is to gain the impression that politics and corn are hard pressed as its main industries by the cultural mechanisms that produce sweetness and light. Iowa goes to bed early but not before it has read an improving book!

Art exhibits ... now find a hearty welcome.

In those Western States where women have assumed the burden of citizenship they seem to lose none of their zeal for art, literature, and music. Equal suffrage was established in Colorado in 1893, and the passing pilgrim cannot fail to be struck by the lack of self-consciousness with which the women of that State discuss social and political questions. The Western woman is animated by a divine energy and she is distinguished by her willingness to render public service. What man neglects or ignores she cheerfully undertakes, and she has so cultivated the gentle art of persuasion that the masculine check-book opens readily to her demand for assistance in her pet causes.

It must not be assumed that in this land of pancakes and panaceas interest in "culture" is new or that its manifestations are sporadic or ill-directed. The early comers brought with them sufficient cultivation to leaven the lump, and the educational forces and cultural movements now everywhere marked in Western communities are but the fruition of the labors of the pioneers who bore books of worth and a love of learning with them into the wilderness. Much sound reading was done in log cabins when the school-teacher was still a rarity, and amid the strenuous labors of the earliest days many sought self-expression in various kinds of writing. Along the Ohio there were bards in abundance, and a decade before the Civil War Cincinnati had honest claims to being a literary centre. The numerous poets of those days—Coggeshall's "Poets and Poetry of the West," published in 1866, mentions one hundred and fifty-two!—were chiefly distinguished by their indifference to the life that lay nearest them. Sentiment and sentimentalism flourished at a time when life was a hard business, though Edward Eggleston is entitled to consideration as an early realist, by reason of "The Hoosier Schoolmaster," which, in spite of Indiana's repudiation of it as false and defamatory, really contains a true picture of conditions with which Eggleston was thoroughly familiar. There followed later E. W. Howe's "The Story of a Country Town" and Hamlin Garland's "Main Travelled Roads," which are landmarks of realism firmly planted in territory invaded later by Romance, bearing the blithe flag of Zenda.

It is not surprising that the Mississippi valley should prove far more responsive to the chimes of romance than to the harsh clang of realism. The West in itself is a romance. Virginia's claims to recognition as the chief field of tourney for romance in America totter before the history of a vast area whose soberest chronicles are enlivened by the most inthralling adventures and a long succession of picturesque characters. The French voyageur, on his way from Canada by lake and river to clasp hands with his kinsmen of the lower Mississippi; the American pioneers, with their own heroes—George Rogers Clark, "Mad Anthony" Wayne, and "Tippecanoe" Harrison; the soldiers of Indian wars and their sons who fought in Mexico in the forties; the men who donned the blue in the sixties; the Knights of the Golden Circle, who kept the war governors anxious in the border States—these are all disclosed upon a tapestry crowded with romantic strife and stress.

The earliest pioneers, enjoying little intercourse with their fellows, had time to fashion many a tale of personal adventure against the coming of a visitor, or for recital on court days, at political meetings, or at the prolonged "camp meetings," where questions of religion were debated. They cultivated unconsciously the art of telling their stories well. The habit of story-telling grew into a social accomplishment and it was by a natural transition that here and there some one began to set down his tales on paper. Thus General Lew Wallace, who lived in the day of great story-tellers, wrote "The Fair God," a romance of the coming of Cortez to Mexico, and followed it with "Ben Hur," one of the most popular romances ever written. Crawfordsville, the Hoosier county-seat where General Wallace lived, was once visited and its romanticism menaced by Mr. Howells, who sought local color for the court scene in "A Modern Instance," his novel of divorce. Indiana was then a place where legal separations were obtainable by convenient processes relinquished later to Nevada.

Maurice Thompson and his brother Will, who wrote "The High Tide at Gettysburg," sent out from Crawfordsville the poems and sketches that made archery a popular amusement in the seventies. The Thompsons, both practising lawyers, employed their leisure in writing and in hunting with the bow and arrow. "The Witchery of Archery" and "Songs of Fair Weather" still retain their pristine charm. That two young men in an Indiana country town should deliberately elect to live in the days of the Plantagenets speaks for the romantic atmosphere of the Hoosier commonwealth. A few miles away James Whitcomb Riley had already begun to experiment with a lyre of a different sort, and quickly won for himself a place in popular affection shared only among American poets by Longfellow. Almost coincident with his passing rose Edgar Lee Masters, with the "Spoon River Anthology," and Vachel Lindsay, a poet hardly less distinguished for penetration and sincerity, to chant of Illinois in the key of realism. John G. Niehardt has answered their signals from Nebraska's corn lands. Nor shall I omit from the briefest list the "Chicago Poems" of Carl Sandburg. The "wind stacker" and the tractor are dangerous engines for Romance to charge: I should want Mr. Booth Tarkington to umpire so momentous a contest. Mr. Tarkington flirts shamelessly with realism and has shown in "The Turmoil" that he can slip overalls and jumper over the sword and ruffles of Beaucaire and make himself a knight of industry. Likewise, in Chicago, Mr. Henry B. Fuller has posted the Chevalier Pensieri-Vani on the steps of the board of trade, merely, we may assume, to collect material for realistic fiction. The West has proved that it is not afraid of its own shadow in the adumbrations of Mrs. Mary A. Watts, Mr. Robert Herrick, Miss Willa Sibert Cather, Mr. William Allen White, and Mr. Brand Whitlock, all novelists of insight, force, and authority; nor may we forget that impressive tale of Chicago, Frank Norris's "The Pit," a work that gains in dignity and significance with the years.

Education in all the Western States has not merely performed its traditional functions, but has become a distinct social and economic force. It is a far cry from the day of the three R's and the dictum that the State's duty to the young ends when it has eliminated them from the illiteracy columns of the census to the State universities and agricultural colleges, with their broad curricula and extension courses, and the free kindergartens, the manual-training high schools, and vocational institutions that are socializing and democratizing education.

IV

In every town of the great Valley there are groups of people earnestly engaged in determined efforts to solve governmental problems. These efforts frequently broaden into "movements" that succeed. We witness here constant battles for reform that are often won only to be lost again. The bosses, driven out at one point, immediately rally and fortify another. Nothing, however, is pleasanter to record than the fact that the war upon vicious or stupid local government goes steadily on and that throughout the field under scrutiny there have been within a decade marked and encouraging gains. The many experiments making with administrative devices are rapidly developing a mass of valuable data. The very lack of uniformity in these movements adds to their interest, in countless communities the attention is arrested by something well done that invites emulation. Constant scandals in municipal administration, due to incompetence, waste, and graft, are slowly penetrating to the consciousness of the apathetic citizen, and sentiment favorable to the abandonment of the old system of partisan local government has grown with remarkable rapidity. The absolute divorcement of municipalities from State and national politics is essential to the conduct of city government on business principles. This statement is made with the more confidence from the fact that it is reinforced by a creditable literature on the subject, illustrated by countless surveys of boss-ridden cities where there is determined protest against government by the unfit. That cities shall be conducted as stock companies with reference solely to the rights and needs of the citizen, without regard to party politics, is the demand in so many quarters that the next decade is bound to witness striking transformations in this field. Last March Kansas City lost a splendidly conducted fight for a new charter that embraced the city-manager plan. Here, however, was a defeat with honor, for the results proved so conclusively the contention of the reformers, that the bosses rule, that the effort was not wasted. In Chicago, Cleveland, Cincinnati, and Minneapolis, the leaven is at work, and the bosses with gratifying density are aiding the cause by their hostility and their constant illustration of the evils of the antiquated system they foster.

The elimination of the saloon in States that have already adopted prohibition promises political changes of the utmost importance in municipal affairs. The saloon is the most familiar and the most mischievous of all the outposts and rallying centres of political venality. Here the political "organization" maintains its faithful sentinels throughout the year; the good citizen, intent upon his lawful business and interested in politics only when election day approaches, is usually unaware that hundreds of barroom loafers are constantly plotting against him. The mounting "dry wave" is attributable quite as much to revolt against the saloon as the most formidable of political units as to a moral detestation of alcohol. Economic considerations also have entered very deeply into the movement, and prohibition advocated as a war measure developed still another phase. The liquor interests provoked and invited the drastic legislation that has overwhelmed their traffic and made dry territory of a large area of the West. By defying regulatory laws and maintaining lobbies in legislatures, by cracking the whip over candidates and office-holders, they made of themselves an intolerable nuisance. Indiana's adoption of prohibition was very largely due to antagonism aroused by the liquor interests through their political activities covering half a century. The frantic efforts of breweries and distilleries there and in many other States to persuade saloon-keepers to obey the laws in the hope of spiking the guns of the opposition came too late. The liquor interests had counselled and encouraged lawlessness too long and found the retailer spoiled by the immunity their old political power had gained for him.

A sweeping Federal law abolishing the traffic may be enacted while these pages are on the press.[A] Without such a measure wet and dry forces will continue to battle; territory that is only partly dry will continue its struggle for bone-dry laws, and States that roped and tied John Barleycorn must resist attempts to put him on his feet again. There is, however, nothing to encourage the idea that the strongly developed sentiment against the saloon will lose its potency; and it is hardly conceivable that any political party in a dry State will write a wet plank into its platform, though stranger things have happened. Men who, in Colorado for example, were bitterly hostile to prohibition confess that the results convince them of its efficacy. The Indiana law became effective last April, and in June the workhouse at Indianapolis was closed permanently, for the interesting reason that the number of police-court prisoners was so reduced as to make the institution unnecessary.

The economic shock caused by the prostration of this long-established business is absorbed much more readily than might be imagined. Compared with other forms of manufacturing, brewing and distilling have been enormously profitable, and the operators have usually taken care of themselves in advance of the destruction of their business. I passed a brewery near Denver that had turned its attention to the making of "near" beer and malted milk, and employed a part of its labor otherwise in the manufacture of pottery. The presence of a herd of cows on the brewery property to supply milk, for combination with malt, marked, with what struck me as the pleasantest of ironies, a cheerful acquiescence in the new order. Denver property rented formerly to saloon-keepers I found pretty generally occupied by shops of other kinds. In one window was this alluring sign:

BUY YOUR SHOES
WHERE YOU BOUGHT YOUR BOOZE

V

The West's general interest in public affairs is not remarkable when we consider the history of the Valley. The pioneers who crossed the Alleghanies with rifle and axe were peculiarly jealous of their rights and liberties. They viewed every political measure in the light of its direct, concrete bearing upon themselves. They risked much to build homes and erect States in the wilderness and they insisted, not unreasonably, that the government should not forget them in their exile. Poverty enforced a strict watch upon public expenditures, and their personal security entered largely into their attitude toward the nation. Their own imperative needs, the thinly distributed population, apprehensions created by the menace of Indians, stubbornly hostile to the white man's encroachments—all contributed to a certain selfishness in the settlers' point of view, and they welcomed political leaders who advocated measures that promised relief and protection. As they listened to the pleas of candidates from the stump (a rostrum fashioned by their own axes!) they were intensely critical. Moreover, the candidate himself was subjected to searching scrutiny. Government, to these men of faith and hardihood, was a very personal thing: the leaders they chose to represent them were in the strictest sense their representatives and agents, whom they retired on very slight provocation.

The sharp projection of the extension of slavery as an issue served to awaken and crystallize national feeling. Education, internal improvements to the accompaniment of wildcat finance, reforms in State and county governments, all yielded before the greater issue. The promise of life, liberty, and the pursuit of happiness had led the venturous husbandmen into woods and prairies, and they viewed with abhorrence the idea that one man might own another and enjoy the fruits of his labor. Lincoln was not more the protagonist of a great cause than the personal spokesman of a body of freemen who were attracted to his standard by the facts of his history that so largely paralleled their own.

It is not too much to say that Lincoln and the struggle of which he was the leader roused the Middle West to its first experience of a national consciousness. The provincial spirit vanished in an hour before the beat of drums under the elms and maples of court-house yards. The successful termination of the war left the West the possessor of a new influence in national affairs. It had not only thrown into the conflict its full share of armed strength but had sent Grant, Sherman, and many military stars of lesser magnitude flashing into the firmament. The West was thenceforth to be reckoned with in all political speculations. Lincoln was the precursor of a line of Presidents all of whom were soldiers: Grant, Hayes, Garfield, Harrison, McKinley; and there was no marked disturbance in the old order until Mr. Cleveland's advent in 1884, with a resulting flare of independence not wholly revealed in the elections following his three campaigns.

My concern here is not with partisan matters, nor even with those internal upheavals that in the past have caused so much heartache to the shepherds of both of the major political flocks. With only the greatest delicacy may one refer to the Democratic schism of 1896 or to the break in the Republican ranks of 1912. But the purposes and aims of the Folks with respect to government are of national importance. The Folks are not at all disposed to relinquish the power in national affairs which they have wielded with growing effectiveness. No matter whether they are right or wrong in their judgments, they are far from being a negligible force, and forecasters of nominees and policies for the future do well to give heed to them.

The trend toward social democracy, with its accompanying eagerness to experiment with new devices for confiding to the people the power of initiating legislation and expelling unsatisfactory officials, paralleled by another tendency toward the short ballot and the concentration of power—these and kindred tendencies are viewed best in a non-partisan spirit in those free Western airs where the electorate is fickle, coy, and hard to please. A good deal of what was called populism twenty years ago, and associated in the minds of the contumelious with long hair and whiskers, was advocated in 1912 by gentlemen who called themselves Progressives and were on good terms with the barber. In the Progressive convention of 1916 I was struck by the great number of Phi Beta Kappa keys worn by delegates and sympathetic spectators. If they were cranks they were educated cranks, who could not be accused of ignorance of the teachings of experience in their political cogitations. They were presumably acquainted with the history of republics from the beginning of time, and the philosophy to be deduced from their disasters. It was because the Progressive party enlisted so many very capable politicians familiar with organization methods that it became a formidable rival of the old parties in 1912. In 1916 it lost most of these supporters, who saw hope of Republican success and were anxious to ride on the bandwagon. Nothing, however, could be more reassuring than the confidence in the people, *i. e.*, the Folks manifested by men and women who know their Plato and are familiar with Isaiah's distrust of the crowd and his reliance upon the remnant.

The isolation of the independent who belongs to no organization and is unaware of the number of voters who share his sentiments, militates against his effectiveness as a protesting factor. He waits timidly in the dark for a flash that will guide him toward some more courageous brother. The American is the most self-conscious being on earth and he is loath to set himself apart to be pointed out as a crank, for in partisan camps all recalcitrants are viewed contemptuously as erratic and dangerous persons. It has been demonstrated that a comparatively small number of voters in half a dozen Western States, acting together, can throw a weight into the scale that will defeat one or the other of the chief candidates for the presidency. If they should content themselves with an organization and, without nominating candidates, menace either side that aroused their hostility, their effectiveness would be increased. But here again we encounter that peculiarity of the American that he likes a crowd. He is so used to the spectacular demonstrations of great campaigns, and so enjoys the thunder of the captains and the shouting, that he is overcome by loneliness when he finds himself at small conferences that plot the overthrow of the party of his former allegiance.

The West may be likened to a naughty boy in a hickory shirt and overalls who enjoys pulling the chair from under his knickerbockered, Eton-collared Eastern cousins. The West creates a new issue whenever it pleases, and wearying of one plaything cheerfully seeks another. It accepts the defeat of free silver and turns joyfully to prohibition, flattering itself that its chief concern is with moral issues. It wants to make the world a better place to live in and it believes in abundant legislation to that end. It experiments by States, points with pride to the results, and seeks to confer the priceless boon upon the nation. Much of its lawmaking is shocking to Eastern conservatism, but no inconsiderable number of Easterners hear the window-smashing and are eager to try it at home.

To spank the West and send it supperless to bed is a very large order, but I have conversed with gentlemen on the Eastern seaboard who feel that this should be done. They go the length of saying that if this chastisement is neglected the republic will perish. Of course, the West doesn't want the republic to perish; it honestly believes itself preordained of all time to preserve the republic. It sits up o' nights to consider ways and means of insuring its preservation. It is very serious and doesn't at all like being chaffed about its hatred of Wall Street and its anxiety to pin annoying tick-tacks on the windows of ruthless corporations. It is going to get everything for the Folks that it can, and it sees nothing improper in the idea of State-owned elevators or of fixing by law the height of the heels on the slippers of its emancipated women. It is in keeping with the cheery contentment of the West that it believes that it has "at home" or can summon to its R. F. D. box everything essential to human happiness.

Across this picture of ease, contentment, and complacency fell the cloud of war. What I am attempting is a record of transition, and I have set down the foregoing with a consciousness that our recent yesterdays already seem remote; that many things that were true only a few months ago are now less true, though it is none the less important that we remember them. It is my hope that what I shall say of that period to which we are even now referring as "before the war" may serve to emphasize the sharpness of America's new confrontations and the yielding, for a time at least, of the pride of sectionalism to the higher demands of nationality.

CHAPTER II
TYPES AND DIVERSIONS

"O I see flashing that this America is only you and me,

Its power, weapons, testimony, are you and me,

Its crimes, lies, thefts, defections, are you and me,

Its Congress is you and me, the officers, capitols, armies, ships, are you and me,

Its endless gestations of new States are you and me,

The war (that war so bloody and grim, the war I will henceforth forget), was you and me,

Natural and artificial are you and me,

Freedom, language, poems, employments, are you and me,

Past, present, future, are you and me."

WHITMAN.

I

AT the end of a week spent in a Middle Western city a visitor from the East inquired wearily: "Does no one work in this town?" The answer to such a question is that of course everybody works; the town boasts no man of leisure; but on occasions the citizens play, and the advent of any properly certified guest affords a capital excuse for a period of intensified sociability. "Welcome" is writ large over the gates of all Western cities—literally in letters of fire at railway-stations. Approaching a town the motorist finds himself courteously welcomed and politely requested to respect the local speed law, and as he departs a sign at the postern thanks him and urges his return. The Western town is distinguished as much by its generous hospitality as by its enterprise, its firm purpose to develop new territory and widen its commercial influence. The visitor is bewildered by the warmth with which he is seized and scheduled for a round of exhausting festivities. He may enjoy all the delights that attend the triumphal tour of a débutante launched upon a round of visits to the girls she knew in school or college; and he will be conscious of a sincerity, a real pride and joy in his presence, that warms his heart to the community. Passing on from one town to another, say from Cincinnati to Cleveland, from Kansas City to Denver, from Omaha to Minneapolis, he finds that news of his approach has preceded him. The people he has met at his last stopping-place have wired everybody they know at the next point in his itinerary to be on the lookout for him, and he finds that instead of entering a strange port there are friends—veritable friends—awaiting him. If by chance he escapes the eye of the reception committee and enters himself on the books of an inn, he is interrupted in his unpacking by offers of lodging in the homes of people he never saw before.

There is no other region in America where so much history has been crowded into so brief a period, where young commonwealths so quickly attained political power and influence as in the Middle West; but the founding of States and the establishment of law is hardly more interesting than the transfer to the wilderness of the dignities and amenities of life. From the verandas of country clubs or handsome villas scattered along the Great Lakes, one may almost witness the receding pageant of discovery and settlement. In Wisconsin and Michigan the golfer in search of an elusive ball has been known to stumble upon an arrow-head, a significant reminder of the newness of the land; and the motorist flying across Ohio, Indiana, and Illinois sees log cabins that survive from the earliest days, many of them still occupied.

Present comfort and luxury are best viewed against a background of pioneer life; at least the sense of things hoped for and realized in these plains is more impressive as one ponders the self-sacrifice and heroism by which the soil was conquered and peopled. The friendliness, the eagerness to serve that are so charming and winning in the West date from those times when one who was not a good neighbor was a potential enemy. Social life was largely dependent upon exigencies that brought the busy pioneers together, to cut timber, build homes, add a barn to meet growing needs, or to assist in "breaking" new acres. The women, eagerly seizing every opportunity to vary the monotony of their lonely lives, gathered with the men, and while the axes swung in the woodland or the plough turned up the new soil, held a quilting, spun flax, made clothing, or otherwise assisted the hostess to get ahead with her never-ending labors. To-day, throughout the broad valley the grandchildren and great-grandchildren of the pioneers ply the tennis-racket and dance in country club-houses beside lakes and rivers where their forebears drove the plough or swung the axe all day, and rode miles to dance on a puncheon floor. There was marrying and giving in marriage; children were born and "raised" amid conditions that cause one to smile at the child-welfare and "better-baby" societies of these times. The affections were deepened by the close union of the family in the intimate association of common tasks. Here, indeed, was a practical application of the dictum of one for all and all for one.

The lines of contact between isolated clearings and meagre settlements were never wholly broken. Months might pass without a household seeing a strange face, but always some one was on the way—an itinerant missionary, a lost hunter, a pioneer looking for a new field to conquer. Motoring at ease through the country, one marvels at the journeys accomplished when blazed trails were the only highways. A pioneer railroad-builder once told me of a pilgrimage he made on horseback from northern Indiana to the Hermitage in Tennessee to meet Old Hickory face to face. Jackson had captivated his boyish fancy and this arduous journey was a small price to pay for the honor of viewing the hero on his own acres. I may add that this gentleman achieved his centennial, remaining a steadfast adherent of Jacksonian democracy to the end of his life. Once I accompanied him to the polls and he donned a silk hat for the occasion, as appropriate to the dignified exercise of his franchise.

There was a distinct type of restless, adventurous pioneer who liked to keep a little ahead of civilization; who found that he could not breathe freely when his farm, acquainted for only a few years with the plough, became the centre of a neighborhood. Men of this sort persuaded themselves that there was better land to be had farther on, though, more or less consciously, it was freedom they craved. The exodus of the Lincolns from Kentucky through Indiana, where they lingered fourteen years before seeking a new home in Illinois, is typical of the pioneer restlessness. In a day when the effects of a household could be moved in one wagon and convoyed by the family on horseback, these transitions were undertaken with the utmost light-heartedness. Only a little while ago I heard a woman of eighty describe her family's removal from Kentucky to Illinois, a wide détour being made that they might visit a distant relative in central Indiana. This, from her recital, must have been the jolliest of excursions, for the children at least, with the daily experiences of fording streams, the constant uncertainties as to the trail, and the camping out in the woods when no cabin offered shelter.

It was a matter of pride with the housewife to make generous provision for "company," and the pioneer annalists dwell much upon the good provender of those days, when venison and wild turkeys were to be had for the killing and corn pone or dodger was the only bread. The reputation of being a good cook was quite as honorable as that of being a successful farmer or a lucky hunter. The Princeton University Press has lately resurrected and republished "The New Purchase," by Baynard Rush Hall, a graduate of Union College and of Princeton Theological Seminary, one of the raciest and most amusing of mid-Western chronicles. Hall sought "a life of poetry and romance amid the rangers of the wood," and in 1823 became principal of Indiana Seminary, the precursor of the State University. Having enjoyed an ampler experience of life than his neighbors, he was able to view the pioneers with a degree of detachment, though sympathetically.

No other contemporaneous account of the social life of the period approaches this for fulness; certainly none equals it in humor. The difficulties of transportation, the encompassing wilderness all but impenetrable, the oddities of frontier character, the simple menage of the pioneer, his food, and the manner of its preparation, and the general social spectacle, are described by a master reporter. One of his best chapters is devoted to a wedding and the subsequent feast, where a huge potpie was the pièce de résistance. He estimates that at least six hens, two chanticleers, and four pullets were lodged in this doughy sepulchre, which was encircled by roast wild turkeys "stuffed" with Indian meal and sausages. Otherwise there were fried venison, fried turkey, fried chicken, fried duck, fried pork, and, he adds, "for anything I knew, even fried leather!"

II

The pioneer adventure in the trans-Mississippi States differed materially from that of the timbered areas of the old Northwest Territory. I incline to the belief that the forest primeval had a socializing effect upon those who first dared its fastnesses, binding the lonely pioneers together by mysterious ties which the open plain lacked. The Southern infusion in the States immediately north of the Ohio undoubtedly influenced the early social life greatly. The Kentuckian, for example, carried his passion for sociability into Indiana, and pages of pioneer history in the Hoosier State might have been lifted bodily from Kentucky chronicles, so similar is their flavor. The Kentuckian was always essentially social; he likes "the swarm," remarks Mr. James Lane Allen. To seek a contrast, the early social picture in Kansas is obscured by the fury of the battle over slavery that dominates the foreground. Other States fought Indians and combated hunger, survived malaria, brimstone and molasses and calomel, and kept in good humor, but the settlement of Kansas was attended with battle, murder, and sudden death. The pioneers of the Northwest Territory began life in amiable accord with their neighbors; Kansas gained Statehood after a bitter war with her sister Missouri, though the contest may not be viewed as a local disturbance, but as a "curtain raiser" for the drama of the Civil War. When in the strenuous fifties Missouri undertook to colonize the Kansas plains with pro-slavery sympathizers, New England rose in majesty to protest. She not only protested vociferously but sent colonies to hold the plain against the invaders. Life in the Kansas of those years of strife was unrelieved by any gayeties. One searches in vain for traces of the comfort and cheer that are a part of the tradition of the settlement of the Ohio valley States. Professor Spring, in his history of Kansas, writes: "For amusement the settlers were left entirely to their own resources. Lectures, concert troupes, and shows never ventured far into the wilderness. Yet there was much broad, rollicking, noisy merrymaking, but it must be confessed that rum and whiskey—lighter liquors like wine and beer could not be obtained—had a good deal to do with it.... Schools, churches, and the various appliances of older civilization got under way and made some growth; but they were still in a primitive, inchoate condition when Kansas took her place in the Union."

There is hardly another American State in which the social organization may be observed as readily as in Kansas. For the reason that its history and the later "social scene" constitute so compact a picture I find myself returning to it frequently for illustrations and comparisons. Born amid tribulation, having indeed been subjected to the ordeal of fire, Kansas marks Puritanism's farthest west; her people are still proud to call their State "The Child of Plymouth Rock." The New Englanders who settled the northeastern part of the Territory were augmented after the Civil War by men of New England stock who had established themselves in Ohio, Illinois, and Iowa when the war began, and having acquired soldiers' homestead rights made use of them to pre-empt land in the younger commonwealth. The influx of veterans after Appomattox sealed the right of Kansas to be called a typical American State. "Kansas sent practically every able-bodied man of military age to the Civil War," says Mr. William Allen White, "and when they came back literally hundreds of thousands of other soldiers came with them and took homesteads." For thirty years after Kansas attained Statehood her New Englanders were a dominating factor in her development, and their influence is still clearly perceptible. The State may be considered almost as one vast plantation, peopled by industrious, aspiring men and women. Class distinctions are little known; snobbery, where it exists, hides itself to avoid ridicule; the State abounds in the "comfortably well off" and the "well-to-do"; millionaires are few and well tamed; every other family boasts an automobile.

While the political and economic results of the Civil War have been much written of, its influence upon the common relationships of life in the border States that it so profoundly affected are hardly less interesting. The pioneer period was becoming a memory, the conditions of life had grown comfortable, and there was ease in Zion when the young generation met a new demand upon their courage. Many were permanently lifted out of the sphere to which they were born and thrust forth into new avenues of opportunity. This was not of course peculiar to the West, though in the Mississippi valley the effects were so closely intermixed with those of the strenuous post-bellum political history that they are indelibly written into the record. Local hostilities aroused by the conflict were of long duration; the copperhead was never forgiven for his disloyalty; it is remembered to this day against his descendants. Men who, in all likelihood, would have died in obscurity but for the changes and chances of war rose to high position. The most conspicuous of such instances is afforded by Grant, whose circumstances and prospects were the poorest when Fame flung open her doors to him.

Nothing pertaining to the war of the sixties impresses the student more than the rapidity with which reputations were made or lost or the effect upon the participants of their military experiences. From farms, shops, and offices men were flung into the most stirring scenes the nation had known. They emerged with the glory of battle upon them to become men of mark in their communities, wearing a new civic and social dignity. It would be interesting to know how many of the survivors attained civil office as the reward of their valor; in the Western States I should say that few escaped some sort of recognition on the score of their military services. In the city that I know best of all, where for three decades at least the most distinguished citizens—certainly the most respected and honored—were veterans of the Civil War, it has always seemed to me remarkable and altogether reassuring as proof that we need never fear the iron collar of militarism, that those men of the sixties so quickly readjusted themselves in peaceful occupations. There were those who capitalized their military achievements, but the vast number had gone to war from the highest patriotic motives and, having done their part, were glad to be quit of it. The shifting about and the new social experiences were responsible for many romances. Men met and married women of whose very existence they would have been ignorant but for the fortunes of war, and in these particulars history was repeating itself last year before our greatest military adventure had really begun!

The sudden appearance of thousands of khaki-clad young men in the summer and fall of 1917 marked a new point of orientation in American life. Romance mounted his charger again; everywhere one met the wistful war bride. The familiar academic ceremonials of college commencements in the West as in the East were transformed into tributes to the patriotism of the graduates and undergraduates already under arms and present in their new uniforms. These young men, encountered in the street, in clubs, in hurried visits to their offices as they transferred their affairs to other hands, were impressively serious and businesslike. In the training-camps one heard familiar college songs rather than battle hymns. Even country-club dances and other functions given for the entertainment of the young soldiers were lacking in light-heartedness. In a Minneapolis country club much affected by candidates for commissions at Fort Snelling, the Saturday-night dances closed with the playing of "The Star-Spangled Banner"; every face turned instantly toward the flag; every hand came to salute; and the effect was to send the whole company, young and old, soberly into the night. In the three training and mobilizing camps that I visited through the first months of preparation—Forts Benjamin Harrison, Sheridan, and Snelling—there was no ignoring the quiet, dogged attitude of the sons of the West, who had no hatred for the people they were enlisted to fight (I heard many of them say this), but were animated by a feeling that something greater even than the dignity and security of this nation, something of deep import to the whole world had called them.

III

In "The American Scene" Mr. James ignored the West, perhaps as lacking in those backgrounds and perspectives that most strongly appealed to him. It is for the reason that "polite society," as we find it in Western cities, has only the scant pioneer background that I have indicated that it is so surprising in the dignity and richness of its manifestations. If it is a meritorious thing for people in prosperous circumstances to spend their money generously and with good taste in the entertainment of their friends, to effect combinations of the congenial in balls, dinners, musicals, and the like, then the social spectacle in the Western provinces is not a negligible feature of their activities. If an aristocracy is a desirable thing in America, the West can, in its cities great and small, produce it, and its quality and tone will be found quite similar to the aristocracy of older communities. We of the West are not so callous as our critics would have us appear, and we are only politely tolerant of the persistence with which fiction and the drama are illuminated with characters whose chief purpose is to illustrate the raw vulgarity of Western civilization. Such persons are no more acceptable socially in Chicago, Minneapolis, or Denver than they are in New York. The country is so closely knit together that a fashionable gathering in one place presents very much the appearance of a similar function in another. New York, socially speaking, is very hospitable to the Southerner; the South has a tradition of aristocracy that the West lacks. In both New York and Boston a very different tone characterizes the mention of a Southern girl and any reference to a daughter of the West. The Western girl may be every bit as "nice" and just as cultivated as the Southern girl: they would be indistinguishable one from the other save for the Southern girl's speech, which we discover to be not provincial but "so charmingly Southern."

Perhaps I may here safely record my impatience of the pretension that provincialism is anywhere admirable. A provincial character may be interesting and amusing as a type; he may be commendably curious about a great number of things and even possess considerable information, without being blessed with the vision to correlate himself with the world beyond the nearest haystack. I do not share the opinion of some of my compatriots of the Western provinces that our speech is really the standard English, that the Western voice is impeccable, or that culture and manners have attained among us any noteworthy dignity that entitles us to strut before the rest of the world. Culture is not a term to be used lightly, and culture, as, say, Matthew Arnold understood it and labored to extend its sphere, is not more respected in these younger States than elsewhere in America. We are offering innumerable vehicles of popular education; we point with pride to public schools, State and privately endowed universities, and to smaller colleges of the noblest standards and aims; but, even with these so abundantly provided, it cannot be maintained that culture in its strict sense cries insistently to the Western imagination. There are people of culture, yes; there are social expressions both interesting and charming; but our preoccupations are mainly with the utilitarian, an attitude wholly defensible and explainable in the light of our newness, the urgent need of bread-winning in our recent yesterdays. However, with the easing in the past fifty years of the conditions of life there followed quite naturally a restlessness, an eagerness to fill and drain the cup of enjoyment, that was only interrupted by our entrance into the world war. There are people, rich and poor, in these States who are devotedly attached to "whatsoever things are lovely," but that they exert any wide influence or color deeply the social fabric is debatable. It is possible that "sweetness and light," as we shall ultimately attain them, will not be an efflorescence of literature or the fine arts, but a realization of justice, highly conceived, and a perfected system of government that will assure the happiness, contentment, and peace of the great body of our citizenry.

In the smaller Western towns, especially where the American stock is dominant, lines of social demarcation are usually obscure to the vanishing-point. Schools and churches are here a democratizing factor, and a woman who "keeps help" is very likely to be apologetic about it; she is anxious to avoid the appearance of "uppishness"—an unpardonable sin. It is impossible for her to ignore the fact that the "girl" in her kitchen has, very likely, gone to school with her children or has been a member of her Sunday-school class. The reluctance of American girls to accept employment as house-servants is an aversion not to be overcome in the West. Thousands of women in comfortable conditions of life manage their homes without outside help other than that of a neighborhood man or a versatile syndicate woman who "comes in" to assist in a weekly cleaning.

There is a type of small-town woman who makes something quite casual and incidental of the day's tasks. Her social enjoyments are in no way hampered if, in entertaining company, she prepares with her own hands the viands for the feast. She takes the greatest pride in her household; she is usually a capital cook and is not troubled by any absurd feeling that she has "demeaned" herself by preparing and serving a meal. She does this exceedingly well, and rises without embarrassment to change the plates and bring in the salad. The salad is excellent and she knows it is excellent and submits with becoming modesty to praise of her handiwork. In homes which it is the highest privilege to visit a joke is made of the housekeeping. The lady of the house performs the various rites in keeping with maternal tradition and the latest approved text-books. You may, if you like, accompany her to the kitchen and watch the broiling of your chop, noting the perfection of the method before testing the result, and all to the accompaniment of charming talk about life and letters or what you will. Corporate feeding in public mess-halls will make slow headway with these strongly individualistic women of the new generation who read prodigiously, manage a baby with their eyes on Pasteur, and are as proud of their biscuits as of their club papers, which we know to be admirable.

Are women less prone to snobbishness than men? Contrary to the general opinion, I think they are. Their gentler natures shrink from unkindness, from the petty cruelties of social differentiation which may be made very poignant in a town of five or ten thousand people, where one cannot pretend with any degree of plausibility that one does not know one's neighbor, or that the daughter of a section foreman or the son of the second-best grocer did not sit beside one's own Susan or Thomas in the public school. The banker's offspring may find the children of the owner of the stave-factory or the planing-mill more congenial associates than the children on the back streets; but when the banker's wife gives a birthday party for Susan the invitations are not limited to the children of the immediate neighbors but include every child in town who has the slightest claim upon her hospitality. The point seems to be established that one may be poor and yet be "nice"; and this is a very comforting philosophy and no mean touchstone of social fitness. I may add that the mid-Western woman, in spite of her strong individualism in domestic matters, is, broadly speaking, fundamentally socialistic. She is the least bit uncomfortable at the thought of inequalities of privilege and opportunity. Not long ago I met in Chicago an old friend, a man who has added greatly to an inherited fortune. To my inquiry as to what he was doing in town he replied ruefully that he was going to buy his wife some clothes! He explained that in her preoccupation with philanthropy and social welfare she had grown not merely indifferent to the call of fashion, but that she seriously questioned her right to adorn herself while her less-favored sisters suffered for life's necessities. This is an extreme case, though I can from my personal acquaintance duplicate it in half a dozen instances of women born to ease and able to command luxury who very sincerely share this feeling.

IV

The social edifice is like a cabinet of file-boxes conveniently arranged so that they may be drawn out and pondered by the curious. The seeker of types is so prone to look for the eccentric, the fantastic (and I am not without my interest in these varieties), which so astonishingly repeat themselves, that he is likely to ignore the claims of the normal, the real "folksy" bread-and-butter people who are, after all, the mainstay of our democracy. They are not to be scornfully waved aside as bourgeoisie, or prodded with such ironies as

Arnold applied to the middle class in England. They constitute the most interesting and admirable of our social strata. There is nothing quite like them in any other country; nowhere else have comfort, opportunity, and aspiration produced the same combination.

The traveller's curiosity is teased constantly, as he cruises through the towns and cities of the Middle West, by the numbers of homes that cannot imaginably be maintained on less than five thousand dollars a year. The economic basis of these establishments invites speculation; in my own city I am ignorant of the means by which hundreds of such homes are conducted—homes that testify to the West's growing good taste in domestic architecture and shelter people whose ambitions are worthy of highest praise. There was a time not so remote when I could identify at sight every pleasure vehicle in town. A man who kept a horse and buggy was thought to be "putting on" a little; if he set up a carriage and two horses he was, unless he enjoyed public confidence in the highest degree, viewed with distrust and suspicion. When in the eighties an Indianapolis bank failed, a cynical old citizen remarked of its president that "no wonder Blank busted, swelling 'round in a carriage with a nigger in uniform"! Nowadays thousands of citizens blithely disport themselves in automobiles that cost several times the value of that banker's equipage. I have confided my bewilderment to friends in other cities and find the same ignorance of the economic foundation of this prosperity. The existence, in cities of one, two, and three hundred thousand people of so many whom we may call non-producers—professional men, managers, agents—offers a stimulating topic for a doctoral thesis. I am not complaining of this phenomenon—I merely wonder about it.

The West's great natural wealth and extraordinary development is nowhere more strikingly denoted than in the thousands of comfortable homes, in hundreds of places, set on forty or eighty foot lots that were tilled land or forest fifty or twenty years ago. Cruising through the West, one enters every city through new additions, frequently sliced out of old forests, with the maples, elms, or beeches carefully retained. Bungalows are inadvertently jotted down as though enthusiastic young architects were using the landscape for sketch-paper. I have inspected large settlements in which no two of these habitations are alike, though the difference may be only a matter of pulling the roof a little lower over the eyes of the veranda or some idiosyncrasy in the matter of the chimney. The trolley and the low-priced automobile are continually widening the urban arc, so that the acre lot or even a larger estate is within the reach of city-dwellers who have a weakness for country air and home-grown vegetables. A hedge, a second barricade of hollyhocks, a flower-box on the veranda rail, and a splash of color when the crimson ramblers are in bloom—here the hunter of types keeps his note-book in hand and wishes that Henry Cuyler Bunner were alive to bring his fine perceptions and sympathies to bear upon these homes and their attractive inmates.

The young woman we see inspecting the mignonette or admonishing the iceman to greater punctuality in his deliveries, would have charmed a lyric from Aldrich. The new additions are, we know, contrived for her special delight. She and her neighbors are not to be confounded with young wives in apartments with kitchenette attached who lean heavily upon the delicatessen-shop and find their sole intellectual stimulus in vaudeville or the dumb drama. It is inconceivable that any one should surprise the mistresses of these bungalows in a state of untidiness, that their babies should not be sound and encouraging specimens of the human race, or that the arrival of unexpected guests should not find their pantries fortified with delicious strawberries or transparent jellies of their own conserving. These young women and their equally young husbands are the product of the high schools, or perhaps they have been fellow students in a State university. With all the world before them where to choose and Providence their guide, they have elected to attack life together and they go about it joyfully. Let no one imagine that they lead starved lives or lack social diversion. Do the housekeepers not gather on one another's verandas every summer afternoon to discuss the care of infants or wars and rumors of wars; and is there not tennis when their young lords come home? On occasions of supreme indulgence the neighborhood laundress watches the baby while they go somewhere to dance or to a play, lecture, or concert in town. They are all musical; indeed, the whole Middle West is melodious with the tinklings of what Mr. George Ade, with brutal impiety, styles "the upright agony box." Or, denied the piano, these habitations at least boast the tuneful disk and command at will the voices of Farrar and Caruso.

V

It is in summer that the Middle Western provinces most candidly present themselves, not only because the fields then publish their richness but for the ease with which the people may be observed. The study of types may then be pursued along the multitudinous avenues in which the Folks disport themselves in search of pleasure. The smoothing-out processes, to which schools, tailors, dressmakers, and "shine-'em" parlors contribute, add to the perils of the type-hunter. Mr. Howells's remark of twenty years ago or more, that the polish slowly dims on footgear as one travels westward, has ceased to be true; types once familiar are so disguised or modified as to be unrecognizable. Even the Western county-seat, long rich in "character," now flaunts the smartest apparel in its shop-windows, and when it reappears in Main Street upon the forms of the citizens one is convinced of the local prosperity and good taste. The keeper of the livery-stable, a stout gentleman, who knows every man, woman, and child in the county and aspires to the shrievalty, has bowed before the all-pervasive automobile. He has transformed his stable into a garage (with a plate-glass "front" exposing the latest model) and hides his galluses (shamelessly exhibited in the day of the horse) under a coat of modish cut, in deference to the sensibilities of lady patrons. The country lawyer is abandoning the trailing frock coat, once the sacred vestment of his profession, having found that the wrinkled tails evoked unfavorable comment from his sons and daughters when they came home from college. The village drunkard is no longer pointed out commiseratingly, local option and State-wide prohibition have destroyed his usefulness as an awful example, and his resourcefulness is taxed to the utmost that he may keep tryst with the skulking bootlegger.

Every town used to have a usurer, a merchant who was "mean" (both of these were frequently pillars in the church), and a dishevelled photographer whose artistic ability was measured by the success of his efforts to make the baby laugh. He solaced himself with the flute or violin between "sittings," not wholly without reference to the charms of the milliner over the way. In the towns I have in mind there was always the young man who would have had a brilliant career but for his passion for gambling, the aleatory means of his destruction being an all-night poker-game in the back room of his law-office opposite the court-house. He may appropriately be grouped with the man who had been ruined by "going security" for a friend, who was spoken of pityingly while the beneficiary of his misplaced confidence, having gained affluence, was execrated. The race is growing better and wiser, and by one means and another these types have been forced from the stage; or perhaps more properly it should be said that the stage and the picture-screen alone seem unaware that they have passed into oblivion.

The Municipal Recreation Pier, Chicago.

The town band remains, however, and it is one of the mysteries of our civilization that virtuosi, capable of performing upon any instrument, exist in the smallest hamlet and meet every Saturday night for practice in the lodge-room over the grocery. I was both auditor and spectator of such a rehearsal one night last summer, in a small town in Illinois. From the garage across the street it was possible to hear and see the artists, and to be aware of the leader's zeal and his stern, critical attitude toward the performers. He seized first the cornet and then the trombone (Hoosierese, sliphorn) to demonstrate the proper phrasing of a difficult passage. The universal Main Street is made festive on summer nights by the presence of the town's fairest daughters, clothed in white samite, mystic, wonderful, who know every one and gossip democratically with their friend the white-jacketed young man who lords it at the druggist's soda-fountain. Such a group gathered and commented derisively upon the experiments of the musicians. That the cornetist was in private life an assistant to the butcher touched their humor; the evocation of melody and the purveying of meat seemed to them irreconcilable. In every such town there is a male quartette that sings the old-time melodies at church entertainments and other gatherings. These vocalists add to the joy of living, and I should lament their passing. Their efforts are more particularly pleasing when, supplemented by guitar and banjo, they move through verdurous avenues thrumming and singing as they go. Somewhere a lattice opens guardedly—how young the world is!

The adventurous boy who, even in times of peace, was scornful of formal education and ran away to enlist in the navy or otherwise sought to widen the cramped horizons of home—and every town has this boy—still reappears at intervals to report to his parents and submit to the admiration and envy of his old schoolmates in the Main Street bazaars. This type endures and will, very likely, persist while there are seas to cross and battles to be won. The trumpetings of war stir the blood of such youngsters, and since our entrance into the war it has been my fortune to know many of them, who were anxious to dare the skies or play with death in the waters under the earth. The West has no monopoly of courage or daring, but it was reassuring to find that the best blood of the Great Valley thrilled to the cry of the bugle. On a railway-train I fell into talk with a young officer of the national army. Finding that I knew the president of the Western college that he had attended, he sketched for me a career which, in view of his twenty-six years, was almost incredible. At eighteen he had enlisted in the navy in the hope of seeing the world, but had been assigned to duty as a hospital orderly. Newport had been one of his stations; there and at other places where he had served he spent his spare hours in study. When he was discharged he signed papers on a British merchant vessel. The ship was short-handed and he was enrolled as an able seaman, which, he said, was an unwarranted compliment, as he proved to the captain's satisfaction when he was sent to the wheel and nearly (as he put it) bowled over a lighthouse. His voyages had carried him to the Orient and the austral seas. After these wanderings he was realizing an early ambition to go to college when the war-drum sounded. He had taken the training at an officer's reserve camp and was on his way to his first assignment. The town he mentioned as his home is hardly more than a whistling-point for locomotives, and I wondered later, as I flashed through it, just what stirring of the spirit had made its peace intolerable and sent him roaming.[B] At a club dinner I met another man, born not far from the town that produced my sailor-soldier, who had fought with the Canadian troops from the beginning of the war until discharged because of wounds received on the French front. His pocketful of medals—he carried them boyishly, like so many marbles, in his trousers pocket!—included the *croix de guerre*, and he had been decorated at Buckingham Palace by King George. He had been a wanderer from boyhood, his father told me, visiting every part of the world that promised adventure and, incidentally, was twice wounded in the Boer War.

The evolution of a type is not, with Mother Nature, a hasty business, and in attempting to answer an inquiry for a definition of the typical mid-Western girl, I am disposed to spare myself humiliating refutations by declaring that there is no such thing. In the Rocky Mountain States and in California, we know, if the motion-picture purveyors may be trusted, that the typical young woman of those regions always wears a sombrero and lives upon the back of a bronco. However, in parts of Ohio, Indiana, and Illinois, where there has been a minimum of intermixture since the original settlements, one is fairly safe in the choice of types. I shall say that in this particular territory the typical young woman is brown-haired, blue or brown of eye, of medium height, with a slender, mobile face that is reminiscent of Celtic influences. Much Scotch-Irish blood flowed into the Ohio valley in the early immigration, and the type survives. In the streets and in public gatherings in Wisconsin and Minnesota the German and Scandinavian infusion is clearly manifest. On the lake-docks and in lumber-camps the big fellows of the North in their Mackinaw coats and close-fitting knit caps impart a heroic note to the landscape. In January, 1917, having gone to St. Paul to witness the winter carnival, I was struck by the great number of tall, fair men who, in their gay holiday attire, satisfied the most exacting ideal of the children of the vikings. They trod the snow with kingly majesty, and to see their performances on skis is to be persuaded that the sagas do not exaggerate the daring of their ancestors.

"What was that?" said Olaf, standing

On the quarter deck.

"Something heard I like the stranding

Of a shattered wreck."

Einar then, the arrow taking

From the loosened string,

Answered "that was Norway breaking

From thy hand, O king!"

The search for characteristic traits is likely to be more fruitful of tangible results than the attempt to fix physical types, and the Western girl who steps from the high schools to the State universities that so hospitably open their doors to her may not be *the* type, but she is indubitably *a* type, well defined. The lore of the ages has been preserved and handed down for her special benefit and she absorbs and assimilates it with ease and grace. Man is no enigma to her; she begins her analysis of the male in high school, and the university offers a post-graduate course in the species. Young men are not more serious over the affairs of their Greek-letter societies than these young women in the management of their sororities, which seem, after school-days, to call for constant reunions. It is not surprising that the Western woman has so valiantly fought for and won recognition of her rights as a citizen. A girl who has matched her wits against boys in the high school and again in a State university, and very likely has surpassed them in scholarship, must be forgiven for assuming that the civil rights accorded them cannot fairly be withheld from her. The many thousands of young women who have taken degrees in these universities have played havoc with the Victorian tradition of womanhood. They constitute an independent, self-assured body, zealous in social and civic service, and not infrequently looking forward to careers.

The State university is truly a well-spring of democracy; this may not be said too emphatically. There is evidence of the pleasantest comradeship between men and women students, and one is impressed in classrooms by the prevailing good cheer and earnestness.

"And one said, smiling, Pretty were the sight

If our old halls could change their sex, and flaunt

With prudes for proctors, dowagers for deans,

And sweet girl-graduates in their golden hair."

Mild flirtations are not regarded as detrimental to the attainment of sound or even distinguished scholarship. The university's social life may be narrow, but it is ampler than that of the farm or "home town." Against the argument that these institutions tend to the promotion of provincial insularity, it may be said that there is a compensating benefit in the mingling of students drawn largely from a single commonwealth. A gentleman whose education was gained in one of the older Eastern universities and in Europe remarked to me that, as his son expected to succeed him in the law, he was sending him to the university of his own State, for the reason that he would meet there young men whose acquaintance would later be of material assistance to him in his profession.

VI

The value of the Great Lakes as a social and recreational medium is hardly less than their importance as commercial highways. The saltless seas are lined with summer colonies and in all the lake cities piers and beaches are a boon to the many who seek relief from the heat which we of the West always speak of defensively as essential to the perfecting of the corn that is our pride. Chicago's joke that it is the best of summer resorts is not without some foundation; certainly one may find there every variety of amusement except salt-water bathing. The salt's stimulus is not missed apparently by the vast number of citizens—estimated at two hundred thousand daily during the fiercest heat—who disport themselves on the shore. The new municipal pier is a prodigious structure, and I know of no place in America where the student of mankind may more profitably plant himself for an evening of contemplation.

**Types and diversions.
A popular bathing beach on Lake Erie, near the town of Sandusky.**

What struck me in a series of observations of the people at play, extending round the lakes from Chicago to Cleveland, was the general good order and decorum. At Detroit I was introduced to two dancing pavilions on the riverside, where the prevailing sobriety was most depressing in view of my promise to the illustrator that somewhere in our pilgrimage I should tax his powers with scenes of depravity and violence. A quarter purchased a string of six tickets, and one of these deposited in a box entitled the owner to take the floor with a partner. As soon as a dance and its several encores was over the floor cleared instantly and one was required to relinquish another ticket. There and in a similar dance-hall in a large Cleveland amusement park fully one-third of the patrons were young women who danced together throughout the evening, and often children tripped into the picture. Chaperonage was afforded by vigilant parents comfortably established in the balcony. The Cleveland resort, accessible to any one for a small fee, interested me particularly because the people were so well apparelled, so "good-looking," and the atmosphere was so charged with the spirit of neighborliness. The favorite dances there were the waltz (old style), the fox-trot, and the schottische. I confess that this recrudescence of the schottische in Cleveland, a progressive city that satisfies so many of the cravings of the aspiring soul—the home of three-cent car-fares and a noble art museum—greatly astonished me. But for the fact that warning of each number was flashed on the wall I should not have trusted my judgment that what I beheld was, indeed, the schottische. Frankly I do not care for the schottische, and it may have been that my tone or manner betokened resentment at its revival; at any rate a policeman whom I interviewed outside the pavilion eyed me with suspicion when I expressed surprise that the schottische was so frequently announced. When I asked why the one-step was ignored utterly he replied contemptuously that no doubt I could find places around Cleveland where that kind of rough stuff was permitted, but "it don't go *here*!" I did not undertake to defend the one-step to so stern a moralist, though it was in his eye that he wished me to do so that he might reproach me for my worldliness. I do not believe he meant to be unjust or harsh or even that he appraised me at once as a seeker of the rough stuff he abhorred; I had merely provided him with an excuse for proclaiming the moral standards of the city of Cleveland, which are high. I made note of the persistence of the Puritan influence in the Western Reserve and hastily withdrew in the direction of the trolley.

Innumerable small lakes lie within the far-flung arms of the major lakes adding variety and charm to a broad landscape, and offering summer refuge to a host of vacationists. Northern Indiana is plentifully sprinkled with lakes and ponds; in Michigan, Wisconsin, and Minnesota there are thousands of them. I am moved to ask—is a river more companionable than a lake? I had always felt that a river had the best of the argument, as more neighborly and human, and I am still disposed to favor those streams of Maine that are played upon by the tides; but an acquaintance with a great number of these inland saucerfuls of blue water has made me their advocate. Happy is the town that has a lake for its back yard! The lakes of Minneapolis (there are ten within the municipal limits) are the distinguishing feature of that city. They seem to have been planted just where they are for the sole purpose of adorning it, and they have been protected and utilized with rare prevision and judgment. To those who would chum with a river, St. Paul offers the Mississippi, where the battlements of the University Club project over a bluff from which the Father of Waters may be admired at leisure, and St. Paul will, if you insist, land you in one of the most delightful of country clubs on the shore of White Bear Lake. I must add that the country club has in the Twin Cities attained a rare state of perfection. That any one should wing far afield from either town in summer seems absurd, so blest are both in opportunities for outdoor enjoyment.

Just how far the wide-spread passion for knitting has interfered with more vigorous sports among our young women I am unable to say, but the loss to links and courts in the Western provinces must have been enormous. The Minikahda Club of Minneapolis was illuminated one day by a girls' luncheon. These radiant young beings entered the dining-room knitting—knitting as gravely as though they were weaving the destinies of nations—and maybe they were! The small confusions and perplexities of seating the party of thirty were increased by the dropping of balls of yarn—and stitches! The round table seemed to be looped with yarn, as though the war overseas were tightening its cords about those young women, whose brothers and cousins and sweethearts were destined to the battle-line.

**On a craft plying the waters of Erie I found all of the conditions of a happy
outing and types that it is always a joy to meet.**

Longfellow celebrated in song "The Four Lakes of Madison," which he apostrophized as "lovely handmaids." I treasure the memory of an approach round one of these lakes to Wisconsin's capitol (one of the few American State-houses that doesn't look like an appropriation!) through a mist that imparted to the dome an inthralling illusion of detachment from the main body of the building. The first star twinkled above it; perhaps it was Wisconsin's star that had wandered out of the galaxy to symbolize for an hour the State's sovereignty!

Whatever one may miss on piers and in amusement parks in the way of types may be sought with confidence on the excursion steamers that ply the lakes—veritable arks in which humanity in countless varieties may be observed. The voyager is satisfied that the banana and peanut and the innocuous "pop" are the ambrosia and nectar of our democracy. Before the boat leaves the dock the deck is littered; one's note-book bristles with memoranda of the untidiness and disorder. On a craft plying the waters of Erie I found all the conditions of a happy outing and types that it is always a joy to meet. The village "cut-up," dashingly perched on the rail; the girl who is never so happy as when organizing and playing games; the young man who yearns to join her group, but is prevented by unconquerable shyness; the child that, carefully planted in the most crowded and inaccessible part of the deck, develops a thirst that results in the constant agitation of half the ship as his needs are satisfied. There is, inevitably, a woman of superior breeding who has taken passage on the boat by mistake, believing it to be first-class, which it so undeniably is not; and if you wear a sympathetic countenance she will confide to you her indignation. The crunching of the peanut-shell, the poignant agony of the child that has loved the banana not wisely but too well, are an affront to this lady. She announces haughtily that she's sure the boat is overcrowded, which it undoubtedly is, and that she means to report this trifling with human life to the authorities. That any one should covet the cloistral calm of a private yacht when the plain folks are so interesting and amusing is only another proof of the constant struggle of the aristocratic ideal to fasten itself upon our continent.

**The Perry monument at Put-in Bay.
A huge column of concrete erected in commemoration
of Commodore Perry's victory.**

Below there was a dining-saloon, but its seclusion was not to be preferred to an assault upon a counter presided over by one of the most remarkable young men I have ever seen. He was tall and of a slenderness, with a wonderful mane of fair hair brushed straight back from his pale brow. As he tossed sandwiches and slabs of pie to the importunate he jerked his hair into place with a magnificent fling of the head. In moments when the appeals of starving supplicants became insistent, and he was confused by the pressure for attention, he would rake his hair with his fingers, and then, wholly composed, swing round and resume the filling of orders. The young man from the check-room went to his assistance, but I felt that he resented this as an impertinence, a reflection upon his prowess. He needed no assistance; before that clamorous company he was the pattern of urbanity. His locks were his strength and his consolation; not once was his aplomb shaken, not even when a stocky gentleman fiercely demanded a whole pie!

While Perry's monument, a noble seamark at Put-in-Bay, is a reminder that the lakes have played their part in American history, it is at Mackinac that one experiences a sense of antiquity. The white-walled fort is a link between the oldest and the newest, and the imagination quickens at the thought of the first adventurous white man who ever braved the uncharted waters; while the eye follows the interminable line of ore barges bound for the steel-mills on the southern curve of Michigan or on the shores of Erie. Commerce in these waters began with the fur-traders travelling in canoes; then came sailing vessels carrying supplies to the new camps and settlements and returning with lumber or produce; but to-day sails are rare and the long leviathans, fascinating in their apparent unwieldiness and undeniable ugliness, are the dominant medium of transportation.

One night, a few years ago, on the breezy terrace of one of the handsomest villas in the lake region, I talked with the head of a great industry whose products are known round the world. His house, furnished with every comfort and luxury, was gay with music and the laughter of young folk. Through the straits crawled the ships, bearing lumber, grain, and ore, signalling their passing in raucous blasts to the lookout at St. Ignace. My host spoke with characteristic simplicity and deep feeling of the poverty of his youth (he came to America an immigrant) and of all that America had meant to him. He was near the end of his days and I have thought often of that evening, of his seigniorial dignity and courtesy, of the portrait he so unconsciously drew of himself against a background adorned with the rich reward of his laborious years. And as he talked it seemed that the power of the West, the prodigious energies of its forests and fields and hills, its enormous potentialities of opportunity, became something concrete and tangible, that flowed in an irresistible tide through the heart of the nation.

CHAPTER III
THE FARMER OF THE MIDDLE WEST

That it may please Thee to give and preserve to our use the kindly fruits of the earth, so that in due time we may enjoy them.—*The Litany*.

WHEN spring marches up the Mississippi valley and the snows of the broad plains find companionship with the snows of yesteryear, the traveller, journeying east or west, is aware that life has awakened in the fields. The winter wheat lies green upon countless acres; thousands of ploughshares turn the fertile earth; the farmer, after the enforced idleness of winter, is again a man of action.

Last year (1917), that witnessed our entrance into the greatest of wars, the American farmer produced 3,159,000,000 bushels of corn, 660,000,000 bushels of wheat, 1,587,000,000 bushels of oats, 60,000,000 bushels of rye. From the day of our entrance into the world struggle against autocracy the American farm has been the subject of a new scrutiny. In all the chancelleries of the world crop reports and estimates are eagerly scanned and tabulated, for while the war lasts and far into the period of rehabilitation and reconstruction that will follow, America must bear the enormous responsibility, not merely of training and equipping armies, building ships, and manufacturing munitions, but of feeding the nations. The farmer himself is roused to a new consciousness of his importance; he is aware that thousands of hands are thrust toward him from over the sea, that every acre of his soil and every ear of corn and bushel of wheat in his bins or in process of cultivation has become a factor in the gigantic struggle to preserve and widen the dominion of democracy.

I

"Better be a farmer, son; the corn grows while you sleep!"

This remark, addressed to me in about my sixth year by my great-uncle, a farmer in central Indiana, lingered long in my memory. There was no disputing his philosophy; corn, intelligently planted and tended, undoubtedly grows at night as well as by day. But the choice of seed demands judgment, and the preparation of the soil and the subsequent care of the growing corn exact hard labor. My earliest impressions of farm life cannot be dissociated from the long, laborious days, the monotonous plodding behind the plough, the incidental "chores," the constant apprehensions as to drought or flood. The country cousins I visited in Indiana and Illinois were all too busy to have much time for play. I used to sit on the fence or tramp beside the boys as they drove the plough, or watch the girls milk the cows or ply the churn, oppressed by an overmastering homesickness. And when the night shut down and the insect chorus floated into the quiet house the isolation was intensified.

My father and his forebears were born and bred to the soil; they scratched the earth all the way from North Carolina into Kentucky and on into Indiana and Illinois. I had just returned, last fall, from a visit to the grave of my grandfather in a country churchyard in central Illinois, round which the corn stood in solemn phalanx, when I received a note from my fifteen-year-old boy, in whom I had hopefully looked for atavistic tendencies. From his school in Connecticut he penned these depressing tidings:

"I have decided never to be a farmer. Yesterday the school was marched three miles to a farm where the boys picked beans all afternoon and then walked back. Much as I like beans and want to help Mr. Hoover conserve our resources, this was rubbing it in. I never want to see a bean again."

I have heard a score of successful business and professional men say that they intended to "make farmers" of their boys, and a number of these acquaintances have succeeded in sending their sons through agricultural schools, but the great-grandchildren of the Middle Western pioneers are not easily persuaded that farming is an honorable calling.

It isn't necessary for gentlemen who watch the tape for crop forecasts to be able to differentiate wheat from oats to appreciate the importance to the prosperous course of general business of a big yield in the grain-fields; but to the average urban citizen farming is something remote and uninteresting, carried on by men he never meets in regions that he only observes hastily from a speeding automobile or the window of a limited train. Great numbers of Middle Western city men indulge in farming as a pastime—and in a majority of cases it is, from the testimony of these absentee proprietors, a pleasant recreation but an expensive one. However, all city men who gratify a weakness for farming are not faddists; many such land-owners manage their plantations with intelligence and make them earn dividends. Mr. George Ade's Indiana farm, Hazelden, is one of the State's show-places. The playwright and humorist says that its best feature is a good nine-hole golf-course and a swimming-pool, but from his "home plant" of 400 acres he cultivates 2,000 acres of fertile Hoosier soil.

A few years ago a manufacturer of my acquaintance, whose family presents a clear urban line for a hundred years, purchased a farm on the edge of a river—more, I imagine, for the view it afforded of a pleasant valley than because of its fertility. An architect entered sympathetically into the business of making habitable a century-old log house, a transition effected without disturbing any of the timbers or the irregular lines of floors and ceilings. So much time was spent in these restorations and readjustments that the busy owner in despair fell upon a mail-order catalogue to complete his preparations for occupancy. A barn, tenant's house, poultry-house, pump and windmill, fencing, and every vehicle and tool needed on the place, including a barometer and wind-gauge, he ordered by post. His joy in his acres was second only to his satisfaction in the ease with which he invoked all the apparatus necessary to his comfort. Every item arrived exactly as the catalogue promised; with the hired man's assistance he fitted the houses together and built a tower for the windmill out of concrete made in a machine provided by the same establishment. His only complaint was that the catalogue didn't offer memorial tablets, as he thought it incumbent upon him to publish in brass the merits of the obscure pioneer who had laboriously fashioned his cabin before the convenient method of post-card ordering had been discovered.

II

Imaginative literature has done little to invest the farm with glamour. The sailor and the warrior, the fisherman and the hunter are celebrated in song and story, but the farmer has inspired no ringing saga or iliad, and the lyric muse has only added to the general joyless impression of the husbandman's life. Hesiod and Virgil wrote with knowledge of farming; Virgil's instructions to the ploughman only need to be hitched to a tractor to bring them up to date, and he was an authority on weather signs. But Horace was no farmer; the Sabine farm is a joke. The best Gray could do for the farmer was to send him homeward plodding his weary way. Burns, at the plough, apostrophized the daisy, but only by indirection did he celebrate the joys of farm life. Wordsworth's "Solitary Reaper" sang a melancholy strain; "Snow-Bound" offers a genial picture, but it is of winter-clad fields. Carleton's "Farm Ballads" sing of poverty and domestic infelicity. Riley made a philosopher and optimist of his Indiana farmer, but his characters are to be taken as individuals rather than as types. There is, I suppose, in every Middle Western county a quizzical, quaint countryman whose sayings are quoted among his neighbors, but the man with a hundred acres of land to till, wood to cut, and stock to feed is not greatly given to poetry or humor.

English novels of rural life are numerous but they are usually in a low key. I have a lingering memory of Hardy's "Woodlanders" as a book of charm, and his tragic "Tess" is probably fiction's highest venture in this field. "Lorna Doone" I remember chiefly because it established in me a distaste for mutton. George Eliot and George Meredith are other English novelists who have written of farm life, nor may I forget Mr. Eden Phillpotts. French fiction, of course, offers brilliant exceptions to the generalization that literature has neglected the farmer; but, in spite of the vast importance of the farm in American life, there is in our fiction no farm novel of distinction. Mr. Hamlin Garland, in "Main Traveled Roads" and in his autobiographical chronicle "A Son of the Middle Border," has thrust his plough deep; but the truth as we know it to be disclosed in these instances is not heartening. The cowboy is the jolliest figure in our fiction, the farmer the dreariest. The shepherd and the herdsman have fared better in all literatures than the farmer, perhaps because their vocations are more leisurely and offer opportunities for contemplation denied the tiller of the soil. The Hebrew prophets and poets were mindful of the pictorial and illustrative values of herd and flock. It is written, "Our cattle also shall go with us," and, journeying across the mountain States, where there is always a herd blurring the range, one thinks inevitably of man's long migration in quest of the Promised Land.

The French peasant has his place in art, but here again we are confronted by joylessness, though I confess that I am resting my case chiefly upon Millet. What Remington did for the American cattle-range no one has done for the farm. Fields of corn and wheat are painted truthfully and effectively, but the critics have withheld their highest praise from these performances. Perhaps a corn-field is not a proper subject for the painter; or it may be that the Maine rocks or a group of birches against a Vermont hillside "compose" better or are supported by a nobler tradition. The most alluring pictures I recall of farm life have been advertisements depicting vast fields of wheat through which the delighted husbandman drives a reaper with all the jauntiness of a king practising for a chariot-race.

I have thus run skippingly through the catalogues of bucolic literature and art to confirm my impression as a layman that farming is not an affair of romance, poetry, or pictures, but a business, exacting and difficult, that may be followed with success only by industrious and enlightened practitioners. The first settlers of the Mississippi valley stand out rather more attractively than their successors of what I shall call the intermediate period. There was no turning back for the pioneers who struck boldly into the unknown, knowing that if they failed to establish themselves and solve the problem of subsisting from the virgin earth they would perish. The battle was to the strong, the intelligent, the resourceful. The first years on a new farm in wilderness or prairie were a prolonged contest between man and nature, nature being as much a foe as an ally. That the social spark survived amid arduous labor and daily self-sacrifice is remarkable; that the earth was subdued to man's will and made to yield him its kindly fruits is a tribute to the splendid courage and indomitable faith of the settlers.

These Middle Western pioneers were in the fullest sense the sons of democracy. The Southern planter with the traditions of the English country gentleman behind him and, in slavery time, representing a survival of the feudal order, had no counterpart in the West, where the settler was limited in his holdings to the number of acres that he and his sons could cultivate by their own labor. I explored, last year, much of the Valley of Democracy, both in seed-time and in harvest. We had been drawn at last into the world war, and its demands and conjectures as to its outcome were upon the lips of men everywhere. It was impossible to avoid reflecting upon the part these plains have played in the history of America and the increasing part they are destined to play in the world history of the future. Every wheat shoot, every stalk of corn was a new testimony to the glory of America. Not an acre of land but had been won by intrepid pioneers who severed all ties but those that bound them to an ideal, whose only tangible expression was the log court-house where they recorded the deeds for their land or the military post that afforded them protection. At Decatur, Illinois, one of these first court-houses still stands, and we are told that within its walls Lincoln often pleaded causes. American democracy could have no finer monument than this; the imagination quickens at the thought of similar huts reared by the axes of the pioneers to establish safeguards of law and order on new soil almost before they had fashioned their habitations. It seemed to me that if the Kaiser had known the spirit in which these august fields were tamed and peopled, or the aspirations, the aims and hopes that are represented in every farmhouse and ranch-house between the Alleghanies and the Rockies, he would not so contemptuously have courted our participation against him in his war for world domination.

What I am calling, for convenience, the intermediate period in the history of the Mississippi valley, began when the rough pioneering was over, and the sons of the first settlers came into an inheritance of cleared land. In the Ohio valley the Civil War found the farmer at ease; to the west and northwest we must set the date further along. The conditions of this intermediate period may not be overlooked in any scrutiny of the farmer of these changed and changing times. When the cloud of the Civil War lifted and the West began asserting itself in the industrial world, the farmer, viewing the smoke-stacks that advertised the entrance of the nearest towns and cities into manufacturing, became a man with a grievance, who bitterly reflected that when rumors of "good times" reached him he saw no perceptible change in his own fortunes or prospects, and in "bad times" he felt himself the victim of hardship and injustice. The glory of pioneering had passed with his father and grandfather; they had departed, leaving him without their incentive of urgent necessity or the exultance of conquest. There may have been some weakening of the fibre, or perhaps it was only a lessening of the tension now that the Indians had been dispersed and the fear of wild beasts lifted from his household.

There were always, of course, men who were pointed to as prosperous, who for one reason or another "got ahead" when others fell behind. They not only held their acres free of mortgage but added to their holdings. These men were very often spoken of as "close," or tight-fisted; in Mr. Brand Whitlock's phrase they were "not rich, but they had money." And, having money and credit, they were sharply differentiated from their neighbors who were forever borrowing to cover a shortage. These men loomed prominently in their counties; they took pride in augmenting the farms inherited from pioneer fathers; they might sit in the State legislature or even in the national Congress. But for many years the farmer was firmly established in the mind of the rest of the world as an object of commiseration. He occupied an anomalous position in the industrial economy. He was a landowner without enjoying the dignity of a capitalist; he performed the most arduous tasks without recognition by organized labor. He was shabby, dull, and uninteresting. He drove to town over a bad road with a load of corn, and, after selling or bartering it, negotiated for the renewal of his mortgage and stood on the street corner, an unheroic figure, until it was time to drive home. He symbolized hard work, hard luck, and discouragement. The saloon, the livery-stable, and the grocery where he did his trading were his only loafing-places. The hotel was inhospitable; he spent no money there and the proprietor didn't want "rubes" or "jays" hanging about. The farmer and his wife ate their midday meal in the farm-wagon or at a restaurant on the "square" where the frugal patronage of farm folk was not despised.

The type I am describing was often wasteful and improvident. The fact that a degree of mechanical skill was required for the care of farm-machinery added to his perplexities; and this apparatus he very likely left out-of-doors all winter for lack of initiative to build a shed to house it. I used to pass frequently a farm where a series of reapers in various stages of decrepitude decorated the barn-lot, with always a new one to heighten the contrast.

The social life of the farmer centred chiefly in the church, where on the Sabbath day he met his neighbors and compared notes with them on the state of the crops. Sundays on the farm I recall as days of gloom that brought an intensification of week-day homesickness. The road was dusty; the church was hot; the hymns were dolorously sung to the accompaniment of a wheezy organ; the sermon was long, strongly flavored with brimstone, and did nothing to lighten

"the heavy and the weary weight

Of all this unintelligible world."

The horses outside stamped noisily in their efforts to shake off the flies. A venturous bee might invade the sanctuary and arouse hope in impious youngsters of an attack upon the parson—a hope never realized! The preacher's appetite alone was a matter for humor; I once reported a Methodist conference at which the succulence of the yellow-legged chickens in a number of communities that contended for the next convocation was debated for an hour. The height of the country boy's ambition was to break a colt and own a side-bar buggy in which to take a neighbor's daughter for a drive on Sunday afternoon.

Community gatherings were rare; men lived and died in the counties where they were born, "having seen nothing, still unblest." County and State fairs offered annual diversion, and the more ambitious farmers displayed their hogs and cattle, or mammoth ears of corn, and reverently placed their prize ribbons in the family Bibles on the centre-tables of their sombre parlors. Cheap side-shows and monstrosities, horse-races and balloon ascensions were provided for their delectation, as marking the ultimate height of their intellectual interests. A characteristic "Riley story" was of a farmer with a boil on the back of his neck, who spent a day at the State fair waiting for the balloon ascension. He inquired repeatedly: "Has the balloon gone up yit?" Of course when the ascension took place he couldn't lift his head to see the balloon, but, satisfied that it really had "gone up," he contentedly left for home. (It may be noted here that the new status of the farmer is marked by an improvement in the character of amusements offered by State-fair managers. Most of the Western States have added creditable exhibitions of paintings to their attractions, and in Minnesota these were last year the subject of lectures that proved to be very popular.)

The farmer, in the years before he found that he must become a scientist and a business man to achieve success, was the prey of a great variety of sharpers. Tumble-down barns bristled with lightning-rods that cost more than the structures were worth. A man who had sold cooking-ranges to farmers once told me of the delights of that occupation. A carload of ranges would be shipped to a county-seat and transferred to wagons. It was the agent's game to arrive at the home of a good "prospect" shortly before noon, take down the old, ramshackle cook-stove, set up the new and glittering range, and assist the womenfolk to prepare a meal. The farmer, coming in from the fields and finding his wife enchanted, would order a range and sign notes for payment. These obligations, after the county had been thoroughly exploited, would be discounted at the local bank. In this way the farmer's wife got a convenient range she would never have thought of buying in town, and her husband paid an exorbitant price for it.

The farmer's wife was, in this period to which I am referring, a poor drudge who appeared at the back door of her town customers on Saturday mornings with eggs and butter. She was copartner with her husband, but, even though she might have "brought" him additional acres at marriage, her spending-money was limited to the income from butter, eggs, and poultry, and even this was dependent upon the generosity of the head of the house. Her kitchen was furnished with only the crudest housewifery apparatus; labor-saving devices reached her slowly. In busy seasons, when there were farm-hands to cook for, she might borrow a neighbor's daughter to help her. Her only relief came when her own daughters grew old enough to assist in her labors. She was often broken down, a prey to disease, before she reached middle life. Her loneliness, the dreary monotony of her existence, the prevailing hopelessness of never "catching up" with her sewing and mending, often drove her insane. The farmhouse itself was a desolate place. There is a mustiness I associate with farmhouses—the damp stuffiness of places never reached by the sun. With all the fresh air in the world to draw from, thousands of farmhouses were ill-lighted and ill-ventilated, and farm sanitation was of the most primitive order.

**A typical old homestead of the Middle West.
The farm on which Tecumseh was born.**

I have dwelt upon the intermediate period merely to heighten the contrast with the new era—an era that finds the problem of farm regeneration put squarely up to the farmer.

III

The new era really began with the passage of the Morrill Act, approved July 2, 1862, though it is only within a decade that the effects of this law upon the efficiency and the character of the farmer have been markedly evident. The Morrill Act not only made the first provision for wide-spread education in agriculture but lighted the way for subsequent legislation that resulted in the elevation of the Department of Agriculture to a cabinet bureau, the system of agriculture experiment-stations, the co-operation of federal and State bureaus for the diffusion of scientific knowledge pertaining to farming and the breeding and care of live-stock, and the recent introduction of vocational training into country schools.

It was fitting that Abraham Lincoln, who had known the hardest farm labor, should have signed a measure of so great importance, that opened new possibilities to the American farmer. The agricultural colleges established under his Act are impressive monuments to Senator Morrill's far-sightedness. When the first land-grant colleges were opened there was little upon which to build courses of instruction. Farming was not recognized as a science but was a form of hard labor based on tradition and varied only by reckless experiments that usually resulted in failure. The first students of the agricultural schools, drawn largely from the farm, were discouraged by the elementary character of the courses. Instruction in ploughing, to young men who had learned to turn a straight furrow as soon as they could tiptoe up to the plough-handles, was not calculated to inspire respect for "book farming" either in students or their doubting parents.

The farmer and his household have found themselves in recent years the object of embarrassing attentions not only from Washington, the land-grant colleges, and the experiment-stations, but countless private agencies have "discovered" the farmer and addressed themselves determinedly to the amelioration of his hardships. The social surveyor, having analyzed the city slum to his satisfaction, springs from his automobile at the farmhouse door and asks questions of the bewildered occupants that rouse the direst apprehensions. Sanitarians invade the premises and recommend the most startling changes and improvements. Once it was possible for typhoid or diphtheria to ravage a household without any interference from the outside world; now a health officer is speedily on the premises to investigate the old oaken bucket, the iron-bound bucket, that hangs in the well, and he very likely ties and seals the well-sweep and bids the farmer bore a new well, in a spot kindly chosen for him, where the barn-lot will not pollute his drinking-water. The questionnaire, dear to the academic investigator, is constantly in circulation. Women's clubs and federations thereof ponder the plight of the farmer's wife and are eager to hitch her wagon to a star. Home-mission societies, alarmed by reports of the decay of the country church, have instituted surveys to determine the truth of this matter. The consolidation of schools, the introduction of comfortable omnibuses to carry children to and from home, the multiplication of country high schools, with a radical revision of the curriculum, the building of two-story schoolhouses in place of the old one-room affair in which all branches were taught at once, and the use of the schoolhouse as a community centre—these changes have dealt a blow to the long-established ideal of the red-mittened country child, wading breast-high through snow to acquaint himself with the three R's and, thus fortified, enter into the full enjoyment of American democracy. Just how Jefferson would look upon these changes and this benignant paternalism I do not know, nor does it matter now that American farm products are reckoned in billions and we are told that the amount must be increased or the world will starve.

The farmer's mail, once restricted to an occasional letter, began to be augmented by other remembrances from Washington than the hollyhock-seed his congressman occasionally conferred upon the farmer's wife. Pamphlets in great numbers poured in upon him, filled with warnings and friendly counsel. The soil he had sown and reaped for years, in the full confidence that he knew all its weaknesses and possibilities, he found to be something very different and called by strange names. His lifelong submission to destructive worms and hoppers was, he learned, unnecessary if not criminal; there were ways of eliminating these enemies, and he shyly discussed the subject with his neighbors.

In speaking of the farmer's shyness I have stumbled into the field of psychology, whose pitfalls are many. The psychologists have as yet played their search-light upon the farm guardedly or from the sociologist's camp. I here condense a few impressions merely that the trained specialist may hasten to convict me of error. The farmer of the Middle West—the typical farmer with approximately a quarter-section of land—is notably sensitive, timid, only mildly curious, cautious, and enormously suspicious. ("The farmer," a Kansas friend whispers, "doesn't vote his opinions; he votes his suspicions!") In spite of the stuffing of his rural-route box with instructive literature designed to increase the productiveness of his acres and lighten his own toil, he met the first overtures of the "book-l'arnin'" specialist warily, and often with open hostility. The reluctant earth has communicated to the farmer, perhaps in all times and in all lands, something of its own stubbornness. He does not like to be driven; he is restive under criticism. The county agent of the extension bureau who seeks him out with the best intentions in the world, to counsel him in his perplexities, must approach him diplomatically. I find in the report of a State director of agricultural extension a discreet statement that "the forces of this department are organized, not for purposes of dictation in agricultural matters but for service and assistance in working out problems pertaining to the farm and the community." The farmer, unaffected as he is by crowd psychology, is not easily disturbed by the great movements and tremendous crises that rouse the urban citizen. He reads his newspaper perhaps more thoroughly than the city man, at least in the winter season when the distractions of the city are greatest and farm duties are the least exacting. Surrounded by the peace of the fields, he is not swayed by mighty events, as men are who scan the day's news on trains and trolleys and catch the hurried comments of their fellow citizens as they plunge through jostling throngs. Professor C. J. Galpin, of Wisconsin University, aptly observes that, while the farmer trades in a village, he shares the invisible government of a township, which "scatters and mystifies" his community sense.

It was a matter of serious complaint that farmers responded very slowly in the first Liberty Loan campaigns. At the second call vigorous attempts were made through the corn belt to rouse the farmer, who had profited so enormously by the war's augmentation of prices. In many cases country banks took the minimum allotment of their communities and then sent for the farmers to come in and subscribe. The Third Loan, however, was met in a much better spirit. The farmer is unused to the methods by which money-raising "drives" are conducted and he resents being told that he must do this, that, or the other thing. Townfolk are beset constantly by demands for money for innumerable causes; there is always a church, a hospital, a social-service house, a Y. M. C. A. building, or some home or refuge for which a special appeal is being made. There is a distinct psychology of generosity based largely on the inspiration of thoroughly organized effort, where teams set forth with a definite quota to "raise" before a fixed hour, but the farmer was long immune from these influences.

In marked contrast with the small farmer, who wrests a scant livelihood from the soil, is his neighbor who boasts a section or a thousand acres, who is able to utilize the newest machinery and to avail himself of the latest disclosures of the laboratories, to increase his profits. One visits these large farms with admiration for the fruitful land, the perfect equipment, the efficient method, and the alert, wide-awake owner. He lives in a comfortable house, often electric-lighted and "plumbed," visits the cities, attends farm conferences, and is keenly alive to the trend of public affairs. If the frost nips his corn he is aware of every means by which "soft" corn may be handled to the best advantage. He knows how many cattle and hogs his own acres will feed, and is ready with cash to buy his neighbors' corn and feed it to stock he buys at just the right turn of the market. It is possible for a man to support himself and a family on eighty acres; I have talked with men who have done this; but they "just about get by." The owner of a big farm, whose modern house and rich demesne are admired by the traveller, is a valued customer of a town or city banker; the important men of his State cultivate his acquaintance, with resulting benefits in a broader outlook than his less-favored neighbors enjoy. Farmers of this class are themselves usually money-lenders or shareholders in country banks, and they watch the trend of affairs from the view-point of the urban business man. They live closer to the world's currents and are more accessible and responsive to appeals of every sort than their less-favored brethren.

But it is the small farmer, the man with the quarter-section or less, who is the special focus of the search-light of educator, scientist, and sociologist. During what I have called the intermediate period—the winter of the farmer's discontent—the politicians did not wholly ignore him. The demagogue went forth in every campaign with special appeals to the honest husbandman, with the unhappy effect of driving the farmer more closely into himself and strengthening his class sense. For the reason that the security of a democracy rests upon the effacement to the vanishing-point of class feeling, and the establishment of a solidarity of interests based upon a common aim and aspiration, the effort making to dignify farming as a calling and quicken the social instincts of the farmer's household are matters of national importance.

It may be said that in no other business is there a mechanism so thoroughly organized for guarding the investor from errors of omission or commission. I am aware of no "service" in any other field of endeavor so excellent as that of the agricultural colleges and their auxiliary experiment and extension branches, and it is a pleasure to testify to the ease with which information touching the farm in all its departments may be collected. Only the obtuse may fail these days to profit by the newest ideas in soil-conservation, plant-nutrition, animal-husbandry, and a thousand other subjects of vital importance to the farmer. To test the "service" I wrote to the Department of Agriculture for information touching a number of subjects in which my ignorance was profound. The return mail brought an astonishing array of documents covering all my inquiries and other literature which my naïve questions had suggested to the Department as likely to prove illuminative. As the extent of the government's aid to the farmer and stockman is known only vaguely to most laymen, I shall set down the titles of some of these publications:

"Management of Sandy Land Farms in Northern Indiana and Southern Michigan."

"The Feeding of Grain Sorghums to Live Stock."

"Prevention of Losses of Live Stock from Plant Poisoning."

"The Feeding of Dairy Cows."

"An Economic Study of the Farm Tractor in the Corn Belt."

"Waste Land and Wasted Land on Farms."

"How to Grow an Acre of Corn."

"How to Select a Sound Horse."

"The Chalcis Fly in Alfalfa Seed."

"Homemade Fireless Cookers and Their Use."

"A Method of Analyzing the Farm Business."

"The Striped Peach Worm."

"The Sheep-Killing Dog."

"Food Habits of the Swallows, a Family of Valuable Native Birds."

As most of these bulletins may be had free and for others only a nominal price of five or ten cents is charged, it is possible to accumulate an extensive library with a very small expenditure. Soil-fertilization alone is the subject of an enormous literature; the field investigator and the laboratory expert have subjected the earth in every part of America to intensive study and their reports are presented clearly and with a minimum use of technical terms. Many manufacturers of implements or materials used on farms publish and distribute books of real dignity in the advertisement of their wares. I have before me a handsome volume, elaborately illustrated, put forth by a Wisconsin concern, describing the proper method of constructing and equipping a dairy-barn. To peruse this work is to be convinced that the manger so alluringly offered really assures the greatest economy of feeding, and the kine are so effectively photographed, so clean, and so contented that one is impelled to an immediate investment in a herd merely for the joy of housing it in the attractive manner recommended by the sagacious advertiser.

Agricultural schools and State extension bureaus manifest the greatest eagerness to serve the earnest seeker for enlightenment. "The Service of YOUR College Brought as Near as Your Mail-Box," is the slogan of the Kansas State Agricultural College. Once upon a time I sought the answer to a problem in Egyptian hieroglyphics and learned that the only American who could speak authoritatively on that particular point was somewhere on the Nile with an exploration party. In the field of agriculture there is no such paucity of scholarship. The very stupidity of a question seems to awaken pity in the intelligent, accommodating persons who are laboring in the farmer's behalf. Augustine Birrell remarks that in the days of the tractarian movement pamphlets were served upon the innocent bystander like sheriffs' processes. In like manner one who manifests only the tamest curiosity touching agriculture in any of its phases will find literature pouring in upon him; and he is distressed to find that it is all so charmingly presented that he is beguiled into reading it!

The charge that the agricultural school is educating students away from the farm is not substantiated by reports from representative institutions of this character. The dean of the College of Agriculture of the University of Illinois, Dr. Eugene Davenport, has prepared a statement illustrative of the sources from which the students of that institution are derived. Every county except two is represented in the agricultural department in a registration of 1,200 students, and, of 710 questioned, 242 are from farms; 40 from towns under 1,000; 87 from towns of 1,000 to 1,500; 262 from towns of 5,000 and up; and 79 from Chicago. Since 1900 nearly 1,000 students have completed the agricultural course in this institution, and of this number 69 per cent are actually living on farms and engaged in farming; 17 per cent are teaching agriculture, or are engaged in extension work; 10 per cent entered callings related to farming, such as veterinary surgery, landscape-gardening, creamery-management, etc.; less than 4 per cent are in occupations not allied with agriculture. It should be explained that the Illinois school had only a nominal existence until seventeen years ago. The number of students has steadily increased from 7 registrations in 1890 to 1,201 in 1916-17. At the Ohio College of Agriculture half the freshman classes of the last three years came from the cities, though this includes students in landscape architecture and horticulture. In Iowa State College the reports of three years show that 54.5 per cent of the freshmen were sons of farmers, and of the graduates of a seven-year period (1907-1914) 34.8 are now engaged in farming.

The opportunities open to the graduates of these colleges have been greatly multiplied by the demand for teachers in vocational schools, and the employment of county agents who must be graduates of a school of agriculture or have had the equivalent in practical farm experience. The influence of the educated farmer upon his neighbors is very marked. They may view his methods with distrust, but when he rolls up a yield of corn that sets a new record for fields with which they are familiar they cannot ignore the fact that, after all, there may be something in the idea of school-taught farming. By the time a farm boy enters college he is sufficiently schooled in his father's methods, and well enough acquainted with the home acres, to appreciate fully the value of the instruction the college offers him.

The only difference between agricultural colleges and other technical schools is that to an unscientific observer the courses in agronomy and its co-ordinate branches deal with vital matters that are more interesting and appealing than those in, let us say, mechanical engineering. If there is something that stirs the imagination in the thought that two blades of grass may be made to grow where only one had grown before, how much more satisfying is the assurance that an acre of soil, properly fertilized and thoroughly tended, may double its yield of corn; that there is a choice well worth the knowing between breeds of beef or dairy cattle, and that there is a demonstrable difference in the energy of foods that may be converted into pork, particularly when there is a shortage and the government, to stimulate hog production, fixes a minimum price (November, 1917) of $15.50 per hundredweight in the Chicago market; and even so stabilized the price is close upon $20 in July, 1918.

Students of agriculture in the pageant that celebrated the fortieth anniversary of the founding of Ohio State University.

The equipment of these institutions includes, with the essential laboratories, farms under cultivation, horses, cattle, sheep, and swine of all the representative breeds. Last fall I spent two days in the agricultural school of a typical land-grant college of the corn belt (Purdue University), and found the experience wholly edifying. The value of this school to the State of Indiana is incalculable. Here the co-ordinate extension service under Professor G. I. Christie is thoroughly systematized, and reaches every acre of land in the commonwealth. "Send for Christie" has become a watchword among Indiana farmers in hours of doubt or peril. Christie can diagnose an individual farmer's troubles in the midst of a stubborn field, and fully satisfy the landowner as to the merit of the prescribed remedy; or he can interest a fashionable city audience in farm problems. He was summoned to Washington a year ago to supervise farm-labor activities, and is a member of the recently organized war policies board.[C] The extension service in all the corn and wheat States is excellent; it must be in capable hands, for the farmer at once becomes suspicious if the State agent doesn't show immediately that he knows his business.

The students at Purdue struck me as more attentive and alert than those I have observed from time to time in literature classes of schools that stick to the humanities. In an entomology class, where I noted the presence of one young woman, attention was riveted upon a certain malevolent grasshopper, the foe of vegetation and in these years of anxious conservation an enemy of civilization. That a young woman should elect a full course in agronomy and allied branches seemed to me highly interesting, and, to learn her habitat in the most delicate manner possible, I asked for a census of the class, to determine how many students were of farm origin. The young lady so deeply absorbed in the grasshopper was, I found, a city girl. Women, it should be noted, are often very successful farmers and stock-breeders. They may be seen at all representative cattle-shows inspecting the exhibits with sophistication and pencilling notes in the catalogues.

To sit in the pavilion of one of these colleges and hear a lecture on the judging of cattle is to be persuaded that much philosophy goes into the production of a tender, juicy beefsteak or a sound, productive milch cow. In a class that I visited a Polled Angus steer and a shorthorn were on exhibition; the instructor might have been a sculptor, conducting a class in modelling, from the nice points of "line," the distribution of muscle and fat, that he dilated upon. He invited questions, which led to a discussion in which the whole class participated. At the conclusion of this lecture a drove of swine was driven in that a number of young gentlemen might practise the fine art of "judging" this species against an approaching competitive meeting with a class from another school. In these days of multiplying farm-implements and tractors, the farmer is driven perforce to know something of mechanics. Time is precious and the breaking down of a harvester may be calamitous if the owner must send to town for some one to repair it. These matters are cared for in the farm-mechanics laboratories where instruction is offered in the care, adjustment, and repair of all kinds of farm-machinery. While in the summer of 1917 only 40,000 tractors were in use on American farms, it is estimated that by the end of the current year the number will have increased to 200,000, greatly minimizing the shortage in men and horses. The substitution of gasolene for horse-power is only one of the many changes in farm methods attributable to the imperative demand for increased production of foodstuffs. Whitman may have foreseen the coming of the tractor when he wrote:

"Well-pleased America, thou beholdest,

Over the fields of the West those crawling monsters;

The human-divine inventions, the labor-saving implements";

for "crawling monster" happily describes the tractor.

The anxiety to serve, to accommodate the instruction to special needs, is illustrated in the length of courses offered, which include a week's intensive course in midwinter designed for farmers, two-year and four-year courses, and post-graduate work. Men well advanced in years attend the midwinter sessions, eager to improve their methods in a business they have followed all their lives. They often bring their wives with them, to attend classes in dairying, poultry-raising, or home economics. It is significant of the new movement in farming that at the University of Wisconsin, an institution whose services to American agriculture are inestimable, there is a course in agricultural journalism, "intended," the catalogue recites, "to be of special service to students who will engage in farming or who expect to be employed in station work or in some form of demonstration or extension service and who therefore may have occasion to write for publication and certainly will have farm produce and products to sell. To these ends the work is very largely confined to studies in agricultural writing."

IV

The easing of the farmer's burdens, through the development of labor-saving machinery, and the convenience of telephones, trolley-lines, and the cheap automobile that have vastly improved his social prospects, has not overcome a growing prejudice against close kinship with the soil. We have still to deal with the loneliness and the social barrenness that have driven thousands of the children of farms to the cities. The son of a small farmer may make a brilliant record in an agricultural college, achieve the distinction of admission to the national honorary agricultural fraternity (the Alpha Zeta, the little brother of the Phi Beta Kappa), and still find the old home crippling and stifling to his awakened social sense.

There is general agreement among the authorities that one of the chief difficulties in the way of improvement is the lack of leadership in farm communities. The farmer is not easily aroused, and he is disposed to resent as an unwarranted infringement upon his constitutional rights the attempts of outsiders to meddle with his domestic affairs. He has found that it is profitable to attend institutes, consult county agents, and peruse the literature distributed from extension centres, but the invasion of his house is a very different matter. Is he not the lord of his acres, an independent, self-respecting citizen, asking no favors of society? Does he not ponder well his civic duty and plot the destruction of the accursed middleman, his arch-enemy? The benevolently inclined who seek him out to persuade him of the error of his ways in any particular are often received with scant courtesy. He must be "shown," not merely "told." The agencies now so diligently at work to improve the farmer's social status understand this and the methods employed are wisely tempered in the light of abundant knowledge of just how much crowding the farmer will stand.

A feeding-plant at "Whitehall," the farm of Edwin S. Kelly, near Springfield, Ohio.

Nothing is so essential to his success as the health of his household; yet inquiries, more particularly in the older States of the Mississippi valley, lead to the conclusion that there is a dismaying amount of chronic invalidism on farms. A physician who is very familiar with farm life declares that "all farmers have stomach trouble," and this obvious exaggeration is rather supported by Dr. John N. Hurty, secretary of the Indiana State Board of Health, who says that he finds in his visits to farmhouses that the cupboards are filled with nostrums warranted to relieve the agonies of poor digestion.

Dr. Hurty, who has probably saved more lives and caused more indignation in his twenty years of public service than any other Hoosier, has made a sanitary survey of four widely separated Indiana counties. In Blackford County, where 1,374 properties were inspected, only 15 per cent of the farmhouses were found to be sanitary. Site, ventilation, water-supply, the condition of the house, and the health of its inmates entered into the scoring. In Ohio County, where 441 homes were visited, 86 per cent were found to be insanitary. The tuberculosis rate for this county was found to be 25 per cent higher than that of the State. In Scott County 97.6 per cent of the farms were pronounced insanitary, and here the tuberculosis rate is 48.3 per cent higher than that of the State. In Union County, where only 2.3 per cent of the farms were found to be sanitary, the average score did not rise above 45 per cent on site, ventilation, and health. Here the tuberculosis death-rate was 176.3 in 100,000, against the State rate of 157. In all these counties the school population showed a decrease.

It should be said that in the communities mentioned, old ones as history runs in this region, many homes stand practically unaltered after fifty or seventy-five years of continuous occupancy. Thousands of farmers who would think it a shameless extravagance to install a bathtub boast an automobile. A survey by Professor George H. von Tungeln, of Iowa College, of 227 farms in two townships of northern Iowa, disclosed 62 bathtubs, 98 pianos, and 124 automobiles. The number of bathtubs reported by the farmers of Ohio is so small that I shrink from stating it.

Here, again, we may be sure that the farmer is not allowed to dwell in slothful indifference to the perils of uncleanliness. On the heels of the sanitarian and the sociologist come the field agents of the home-economics departments of the meddlesome land-grant colleges, bent upon showing him a better way of life. I was pondering the plight of the bathless farmhouse when a document reached me showing how a farmhouse may enjoy running water, bathroom, gas, furnace, and two fireplaces for an expenditure of $723.97. One concrete story is better than many treatises, and I cheerfully cite, as my authority, "Modernizing an Old Farm House," by Mrs. F. F. Showers, included among the publications of the Wisconsin College of Agriculture. The home-economics departments do not wait for the daughters of the farm to come to them, but seek them out with the glad tidings that greater ease and comfort are within their reach if only their fathers can be made to see the light. In many States the extension agents organize companies of countrywomen and carry them junketing to modern farmhouses.

Turning to Nebraska, whose rolling cornfields are among the noblest to be encountered anywhere, home-demonstration agents range the commonwealth organizing clubs, which are federated where possible to widen social contacts, better-babies conferences, and child-welfare exhibits.

The Community Welfare Assembly, as conducted in Kansas, has the merit of offering a varied programme—lectures on agriculture and home economics, civics, health, and rural education by specialists, moving pictures, community music, and folk games and stories for the children. In Wisconsin the rural-club movement reaches every part of the State, and a State law grants the use of schoolhouses for community gatherings. Seymour, Indiana, boasts a Farmer's Club, the gift of a citizen, with a comfortably appointed house, where farmers and their families may take their ease when in town.

The organization of boys' and girls' clubs among farm youth is a feature of the vocational-training service offered under the Smith-Lever Act of 1914, and already the reports of its progress are highly interesting. These organizations make possible the immediate application of the instruction in agriculture and home economics received in the schools. In Indiana more than 25,000 boys and girls were enlisted last year in such club projects as the cultivation of corn, potatoes, and garden vegetables, canning, sewing, and home-craft, and the net profit from these sources was $105,100. In my prowlings nothing has delighted me more than the discovery of the Pig Club. This is one of Uncle Sam's many schemes for developing the initiative and stimulating the ambition of farm children. It might occur to the city boy, whose acquaintance with pork is limited to his breakfast bacon, that the feeding of a pig is not a matter worthy of the consideration of youth of intelligence and aspiration. Uncle Sam, however, holds the contrary opinion. From a desk in the Department of Agriculture he has thrown a rosy glamour about the lowly pig. Country bankers, properly approached and satisfied of the good character and honorable intentions of applicants, will advance money to farm boys to launch them upon pig-feeding careers. My heart warms to Douglas Byrne, of Harrison County, Indiana, who, under the guidance of a club supervisor, fed 17 hogs with a profit of $99.30. Another young Hoosier, Elmer Pearce, of Vanderburgh County, fed 2 pigs that made a daily gain of 1.38 pounds for four months, and sold them at a profit of $12.36. We learn from the official report that this young man's father warned him that the hogs he exercised his talents upon would make no such gains as were achieved. Instead of spanking the lad for his perverseness, as would have been the case in the olden golden days, this father made him the ruler over 30 swine. There are calf and pig clubs for girls, and a record has been set for Indiana by twelve-year-old Pauline Hadley, of Mooresville, who cared for a Poland China hog for 110 days, increasing its weight from 65 to 256 pounds, and sold it at a profit of $20.08.

The farmer of yesterday blundered through a year and at the end had a very imperfect idea of his profits and losses. He kept no accounts; if he paid his taxes and the interest on the omnipresent mortgage, and established credit for the winter with his grocer, he was satisfied. Uncle Sam, thoroughly aroused to the importance of increasing the farmer's efficiency, now shows him how to keep simple accounts and returns at the end of the season to analyze the results. (Farm-management is the subject of many beguiling pamphlets; it seems incredible that any farmer should blindly go on wasting time and money when his every weakness is anticipated and prescribed for by the Department of Agriculture and its great army of investigators and counsellors!)

If there is little cheerful fiction dealing with farm life, its absence is compensated for by the abundance of "true stories" of the most stimulating character, to be found in the publications of the State agricultural extension bureaus. Professor Christie's report of the Indiana Extension Service for last year recites the result of three years' observation of a southern Indiana farm of 213 acres. In 1914 the owner cleared $427 above interest on his capital, in addition to his living. This, however, was better than the average for the community, which was a cash return of $153. This man had nearly twice as much land as his neighbors, carried more live-stock, and his crop yields were twice as great as the community average. His attention was called to the fact that he was investing $100 worth of feed and getting back only $82 in his live-stock account. He was expending 780 days in the care of his farm and stock, which the average corn-belt farmer could have managed with 605 days of labor. Acting on the advice of the Extension Department, he added to his live-stock, built a silo, changed his feeding ration, and increased his live-stock receipts to $154 per $100 of feed. The care of the additional live-stock through the winter resulted in a better reward for his labor and the amount accredited to labor income for the year was $1,505. The third year he increased his live-stock and poultry, further improved the feeding ration, and received $205 per $100 of feed. By adding to the conveniences of his barn, he was able to cut down his expenditure for hired labor; or, to give the exact figures, he reduced the amount expended in this way from $515 to $175. His labor income for the third year was $3,451. "Labor income," as the phrase is employed in farm bookkeeping, is the net sum remaining after the farm-owner has paid all business expenses of the farm and deducted a fair interest on the amount invested in his plant.

I have mentioned the 80-acre farm as affording a living for a family; but there is no ignoring the testimony of farm-management surveys, covering a wide area, that this unit is too small to yield the owner the best results from his labor. In a Nebraska survey it is demonstrated that farms of from 200 to 250 acres show better average returns than those of larger or smaller groups, but rainfall, soil conditions, and the farmer's personal qualifications are factors in all such studies that make generalizations difficult. A diversified farm of 160 acres requires approximately 3,000 hours' labor a year. Forty-five acres of corn, shocked and husked, consume 270 days of labor; like acreages of oats and clover, 90 and 45 days respectively; care of live-stock and poultry, 195 days. In summer a farmer often works twelve or fourteen hours a day, while in winter, with only his stock to look after, his labor is reduced to three or four hours.

The Smith-Hughes Act (approved February, 1917) appropriates annually sums which will attain, in 1926, a maximum of $3,000,000 "for co-operation with the States in the promotion of education in agriculture and the trades and industries, and in the preparation of teachers of vocational subjects, the sums to be allotted to the States in the proportion which their rural population bears to the total rural population of the United States." Washington is only the dynamic centre of inspiration and energy in the application of the laws that make so generous provision for the farmer's welfare. The States must enter into a contract to defray their share of the expense and put the processes into operation.

There was something of prophecy in the message of President Roosevelt (February 9, 1909) transmitting to Congress the report of his Country Life Commission. He said: "Upon the development of country life rests ultimately our ability, by methods of farming requiring the highest intelligence, to continue to feed and clothe the hungry nations; to supply the city with fresh blood, clean bodies, and clear brains that can endure the terrific strain of modern life; we need the development of men in the open country, who will be in the future, as in the past, the stay and strength of the nation in time of war, and its guiding and controlling spirit in time of peace." The far-reaching effect of the report, a remarkably thorough and searching study of farm conditions, is perceptible in agencies and movements that were either suggested by it or that were strengthened by its authoritative utterances.

V

Much has been written of the decline of religion in rural communities, and melancholy statistics have been adduced as to the abandonment of churches. But here, as in the matter of farm efficiency and kindred rural problems, vigorous attempts are making to improve conditions. "The great spiritual needs of the country community just at present are higher personal and community ideals," the Country Life Commission reported. "Rural people have need to have an aspiration for the highest possible development of the community. There must be an ambition on the part of the people themselves constantly to progress in all those things that make the community life wholesome, satisfying, educative, and complete. There must be a desire to develop a permanent environment for the country boy and girl, of which they will become passionately fond. As a pure matter of education, the countryman must learn to love the country and to have an intellectual appreciation of it." In this connection I wish that every farm boy and girl in America might read "The Holy Earth," by L. H. Bailey (a member of the commission), a book informed with a singular sweetness and nobility, and fit to be established as an auxiliary reading-book in every agricultural college in America.

There is abundant evidence that the religious bodies are not indifferent to the importance of vitalizing the country church, and here the general socializing movement is acting as a stimulus. Not only have the churches, in federal and State conferences, set themselves determinedly to improve the rural parish, but the matter has been the subject of much discussion by educational and sociological societies with encouraging gains. The widespread movement for the consolidation of country schools suggests inevitably the combination of country parishes, assuring greater stability and making possible the employment of permanent ministers of a higher intellectual type, capable of exercising that intelligent local leadership which all commentators on the future of the farm agree is essential to progress.

By whatever avenue the rural problem is approached it is apparent that it is not sufficient to persuade American youth of the economic advantages of farming over urban employments, but that the new generation must be convinced in very concrete ways that country life affords generous opportunities for comfort and happiness, and that there are compensations for all it lacks. The farmer of yesterday, strongly individualistic and feeling that the world's rough hand was lifted against him, has no longer an excuse for holding aloof from the countless forces that are attempting to aid him and give his children a better chance in life. No other figure in the American social picture is receiving so much attention as the farmer. A great treasure of money is expended annually by State and federal governments to increase his income, lessen his labor, educate his children, and bring health and comfort to his home. If he fails to take advantage of the vast machinery that is at work in his behalf, it is his own fault; if his children do not profit by the labors of the State to educate them, the sin is at his own door. In his business perplexities he has but to telephone to a county agent or to the extension headquarters of his State to receive the friendly counsel of an expert. If his children are dissatisfied and long for variety and change, it is because he has concealed from them the means by which their lives may be quickened and brightened.

Judging graded shorthorn herds at the American Royal Live Stock Show in Kansas City.

With the greatest self-denial I refrain from concluding this chapter with a ringing peroration in glorification of farm life. From a desk on the fifteenth floor of an office-building, with an outlook across a smoky, clanging industrial city, I could do this comfortably and with an easy conscience. But the scientist has stolen farming away from the sentimentalist and the theorist. Farming, I may repeat, is a business, the oldest and the newest in the world. No year passes in which its methods and processes are not carried nearer to perfection. City boys now about to choose a vocation will do well to visit an agricultural college and extension plant, or, better still, a representative corn-belt farm, before making the momentous decision. Perhaps the thousands of urban lads who this year volunteered to aid the farmers as a patriotic service will be persuaded that the soil affords opportunities not lightly to be passed by. No one can foretell the vast changes that will be precipitated when the mighty war is ended; but one point is undebatable: the world, no matter how low its fortunes may sink, must have bread and meat. Tremendous changes and readjustments are already foreshadowed; but in all speculations the productiveness of the American farm will continue to be a factor of enormous importance.

A wide-spread absorption of land by large investors, the increase of tenantry, and the passing of the farm family are possibilities of the future not to be overlooked by those who have at heart the fullest and soundest development of American democracy. For every 100 acres of American land now under cultivation there are about 375 acres untilled but susceptible of cultivation. Here is a chance for American boys of the best fibre to elect a calling that more and more demands trained intelligence. All things considered, the rewards of farming average higher than those in any other occupation, and the ambitious youth, touched with the new American passion for service, for a more perfect realization of the promise of democracy, will find in rural communities a fallow field ready to his hand.

CHAPTER IV
CHICAGO

"And yonder where, gigantic, wilful, young,

Chicago sitteth at the northwest gates,

With restless violent hands and casual tongue

Moulding her mighty fates——"

WILLIAM VAUGHN MOODY.

I

A FATEFUL Titan, brooding over a mammoth chess-board, now cautious in his moves as he shifts his myriad pigmies, now daring, but always resolute, clear-eyed, steady of hand, and with no thought but victory—as such a figure Rodin might have visualized twentieth-century Chicago.

Chicago is not a baby and utters no bleating cry that it is "misunderstood," and yet a great many people have not only misunderstood or misinterpreted it but have expressed their dislike with hearty frankness. To many visitors Chicago is a city of dreadful night, to be explored as hurriedly as possible with outward-bound ticket clenched tightly in hand. But Chicago may not be comprehended in the usual scamper of the tourist; for the interesting thing about this city is the people, and they require time. I do not, of course, mean that they are all worthy of individual scrutiny, but rather that the very fact of so many human beings collecting there, living cheerfully and harmoniously, laboring and aspiring and illustrating the pressing, changing problems of our democracy awakens at once the beholder's sympathetic interest. Chicago is not New York, nor is it London or Paris: Chicago is different. The Chicagoan will convince you of this if you fail to see it; the point has been conceded by a great number of observers from all quarters, but not in just the same spirit in which the citizen speaks of it.

Both inspired and uninspired critics have made Chicago the subject of a considerable literature that runs the gamut of anxious concern, dismal apprehension, dismay, and disgust. Mr. Kipling saw the city embodied as a girl arrayed in a costume of red and black, shod in red shoes sauntering jauntily down the gory aisle of a slaughter-house. Mr. H. G. Wells boasts that he refrained from visiting the packing-houses owing to what he describes as his immense "repugnance to the killing of fixed and helpless animals." He reports that he saw nothing of those "ill-managed, ill-inspected establishments," though he "smelt the unwholesome reek from them over and over again," and observed with trepidation "the enormous expanse and intricacy of railroads that net this great industrial desolation." Chicago's pressing need, he philosophizes, is discipline—a panacea which he generously prescribes not only for all that displeased him in America, but for Lancashire, South and East London, and the Pas de Calais. "Each man," he ruminates, "is for himself, each enterprise; there is no order, no prevision, no common and universal plan." I have cheerfully set down this last statement to lighten my own burdens, for by reversing it one may very happily express the real truth about Chicago. Instead of the "shoving unintelligent proceedings of under-bred and morally obtuse men," great numbers of men and women of the highest intelligence are constantly directing their talents toward the amelioration of the very conditions that grieved Mr. Wells.

Chicago may, to be sure, be dismissed in a few brilliant phrases as the black pit of perdition, the jumping-off place of the world; but to the serious-minded American the effort making there for the common uplift is too searching, too intelligent, too sincere, for sneers. I fancy that in view of events that have occurred in Europe since his visit to America Mr. Wells would be less likely to rest his case against Chicago on the need of discipline alone. All that discipline may do for a people had been achieved by the Imperial German Government when the Kaiser started for Paris in 1914; but subjection, obedience, even a highly developed efficiency are not the whole of the law and the prophets. Justice and mercy are finer things, and nothing in Chicago is more impressive or encouraging than the stubborn purpose of many citizens who are neither foolish nor ignorant to win and establish these twain for the whole. It is an unjust and ungenerous assumption that Chicago is unaware of its needs and dangers, or that from year to year no gains are made in the attempt to fuse and enlighten the mass. It is the greatest laboratory that democracy has known. The very fact that so much effort must go into experiment, that there are more than two and a half million distinct units to deal with, with a resulting confusion in needs and aims, adds not merely to the perplexity but to the fascination of the social and political enigma. There is, quite definitely, a thing called the Chicago spirit, a thing compounded of energy, faith, and hope—and again energy! Nor is the energy all spent upon the material and sordid, for the fine, arresting thing is the tremendous vim this lusty young giant among the world's cities brings to the solution of its problems—problems that deserve to be printed in capitals out of respect for their immensity and far-reaching importance to the national life. Chicago does not walk around her problems, but meets them squarely and manfully. The heart of the inquirer is won by the perfect candor with which the Chicagoan replies to criticism; the critic is advised that for every evil there is a remedy; indeed, that some agency is at work on that particular thing at that particular moment. This information is conveyed with a smile that expresses Chicago's faith and hope—a smile that may be a little sad and wistful—but the faith and the hope are inescapably there.

Chicago is the industrial and financial clearing-house, the inspirational centre of the arts, and the playground for 50,000,000 people. The pilgrim who lands on the lake shore with an open mind and a fair understanding of what America is all about—the unprejudiced traveller—is immediately conscious that here, indeed, is a veritable capital of democracy.

Every night three hundred or more sleeping-cars bear approximately 4,500 persons toward this Western metropolis on journeys varying from five to twelve hours in length. From innumerable points it is a night's run, and any morning one may see these pilgrims pouring out of the railway-stations, dispersing upon a thousand errands, often concluded in time for the return trip between six o'clock and midnight. At times one wonders whether all the citizens of the tributary provinces have not gathered here at once, so great is the pressure upon hotel space, so thronged the streets. The sleeping-car holds no terrors for the Westerner. He enjoys the friendship of the train-crews; the porters—many of them veterans of the service—call him by name and in addressing them he avoids the generic "George," which the travelling salesman applies to all knights of the whisk-broom, and greets them by their true baptismal appellations of Joshua or Obadiah. Mr. George Ade has threatened to organize a "Society for the Prevention of the Calling of Sleeping-Car Porters George"!

The professional or business man rises from his meagre couch refreshed and keen for adventure and, after a strenuous day, returns to it and slumbers peacefully as he is hurled homeward. The man from Sioux City or Saint Joe who spends a day here does not crawl into his berth weary and depressed, but returns inspired and cheered and determined to put more vim into his business the next morning. On the homeward trail, eating supper in company with the neighbors he finds aboard, he dilates eloquently upon the wonders of the city, upon its enterprise, upon the heartiness with which its business men meet their customers. Chicago men work longer hours than their New York brethren and take pride in their accessibility. It is easier to get a hearing in high quarters in any field of endeavor in Chicago than in New York; there is less waiting in the anteroom, and a better chance of being asked out for lunch.

The West is proud of Chicago and loves it with a passionate devotion. Nor is it the purpose of these reflections to hint that this mighty Mecca is unworthy of the adoration of the millions who turn toward it in affection and reverence. Chicago not only draws strength from a vast territory but, through myriad agencies and avenues, sends back a mighty power from its huge dynamo. It is the big brother of all lesser towns, throwing an arm about Davenport and Indianapolis, Springfield and Columbus, and manifesting a kindly tolerance toward St. Louis, Kansas City, Detroit, Minneapolis, and Cleveland, whose growth and prosperity lift them to a recognized and respected rivalry.

Chicago is the big brother of all lesser towns.

The intense loyalty of the Chicagoan to his city is one of his most admirable characteristics and the secret of his city's greatness. He is proud even of the Chicago climate, which offers from time to time every variety of weather known to meteorology and is capable of effecting combinations utterly new to this most fascinating of sciences. Chicago's coldest day of record was in 1872, when the minus registration was 23; the hottest in 1901, when the mercury rose to 103. Such excesses are followed by contrition and repentance and days of ethereal mildness. The lake serves as a funnel down which roar icy blasts direct from the hyperboreans. The wind cuts like a scythe of ice swung by a giant. In summer the hot plains pour in their burning heat; or, again, when it pleases the weather-god to produce a humid condition, the moisture-charged air is stifling. But a Chicagoan does not mind the winter, which he declares to be good for body and soul; and, as for the heat, he maintains—and with a degree of truth to sustain him—that the nights are always cool. The throngs that gathered in Chicago for the Republican and the Progressive conventions in June, 1916, were treated to a diversity of weather, mostly bad. It was cold; it rained hideously. There were dismal hours of waiting for reports of the negotiations between the two bodies of delegates in which the noblest oratory failed to bring warmth and cheer. Chicago did her worst that week, but without serious impairment of her prestige as the greatest convention city in the world. Every one said, "Isn't this just like Chicago!" and inquired the way to the nearest quinine.

"The Windy City" is a descriptive sobriquet. There are not only cold winds and hot winds of the greatest intensity, but there are innumerable little gusts that spring up out of nowhere for no other conceivable purpose than to deposit dust or cinders in the human eye. There is a gesture acquired by all Chicagoans—a familiar bit of calisthenics essential to the preservation of head-gear. If you see a man pursuing his hat in a Chicago street you may be sure that he is an outsider; the native knows by a kind of prescience just when the fateful breeze is coming, prepares for it, and is never caught unawares. In like manner the local optic seems to be impregnable to persistent attacks of the omnipresent cinder. By what means the eyeball of a visitor becomes the haven for flying débris, while the native-born walks unscathed, is beyond my philosophy. It must be that the eye of the inhabitant is trained to resist these malevolent assaults and that the sharp-edged cinder spitefully awaits an opportunity to impinge upon the defenseless optic of passing pilgrims. The pall of smoke miraculously disappears at times and the cinder abandons its depredations. The sky may be as blue over Chicago as anywhere else on earth. The lake shimmers like silk and from brown, near shore, runs away to the horizon through every tint of blue and green and vague, elusive purples.

II

Chicago still retained, in the years of my first acquaintance, something of the tang of the wild onion which in the Indian vernacular was responsible for its name. (I shudderingly take refuge in this parenthesis to avoid collision with etymological experts who have spent their lives sherlocking the word's origin. The genesis of "Chicago" is a moot question, not likely to be settled at this late day. Whether it meant leek, polecat, skunkweed, or onion does not greatly matter. I choose the wild onion from the possibilities, for the highly unscientific reason that it seems to me the most appropriate and flavorsome of all accessible suggestions.)

In the early eighties one might stand by the lakeside and be very conscious of a West beyond that was still in a pioneer stage. At the department headquarters of the army might be met hardy campaigners against the Indians of mountain and plain who were still a little apprehensive that the telegraph might demand orders for the movement of troops against hostile red men along the vanishing frontiers. The battle of Wounded Knee, in which 100 warriors and 120 women and children were found dead on the field (December 29, 1890), might almost have been observed from a parlor-car window. It may have been that on my visits I chanced to touch circles dominated by Civil War veterans, but great numbers of these diverted their energies to peaceful channels in Chicago at the end of the rebellion, and they gave color to the city life. It was a part of the upbringing of a mid-Western boy of my generation to reverence the heroes of the sixties, and it was fitting that in the land of Lincoln and in a State that gave Grant a regiment and started him toward immortality there should be frequent reunions of veterans, and political assemblages and agitations in which they figured, to encourage hero-worship in the young. Unforgettable among the more distinguished of these Civil War veterans was General John A. Logan, sometime senator in Congress and Blaine's running mate in 1884. In life he was a gallant and winning figure, and Saint Gaudens's equestrian statue in Grant Park preserves his memory in a city that delighted to honor him.

Chicago's attractions in those days included summer engagements of Theodore Thomas's orchestra, preceding Mr. Thomas's removal to the city and the founding of the orchestra that became his memorial. Concerts were given in an exposition hall on the site now occupied by the Art Institute, with railway-trains gayly disporting on the lake side of the building. So persistent is the association of ideas, that to this day I never hear the Fifth Symphony or the Tannhäuser Overture free of the rumble and jar and screech of traffic. It was in keeping with Chicago's good-humored tolerance of the incongruous and discordant in those years that the scores of Beethoven and Wagner should be punctuated by locomotive whistles, and that *pianissimo* passages should be drowned in the grinding of brakes.

At this period David Swing stood every Sunday morning in Central Music Hall addressing large audiences, and he looms importantly in the Chicago of my earliest knowledge. Swing was not only a fine classical scholar—he lectured charmingly on the Greek poets—but he preached a gospel that harmonized with the hopeful and liberal Chicago spirit as it gathered strength and sought the forms in which it has later declared itself. He was not an orator in the sense that Ingersoll and Beecher were; as I remember, he always read his sermons or addresses; but he was a strikingly individual and magnetic person, whose fine cultivation shone brilliantly in his discourses. In the retrospect it seems flattering to the Chicago of that time that it recognized and appreciated his quality in spite of an unorthodoxy that had caused his retirement from the formal ministry.

The third member of a trinity that lingers agreeably in my memory is Eugene Field. Journalism has known no more versatile genius, and his column of "Sharps and Flats" in the *Morning News* (later the *Record*) voiced the Chicago of his day. Here indubitably was the flavor of the original wild-onion beds of the Jesuit chronicles! Field became an institution quite as much as Thomas and Swing, and reached an audience that ultimately embraced the whole United States. The literary finish of his paragraphs, their wide range of subject, their tone, varying from kindly encouraging comment on a new book of verse that had won his approval to a mocking jibe at some politician, his hatred of pretense, the plausibility of the hoaxes he was constantly perpetrating, gave an infinite zest to his department. The most devoted of Chicagoans, he nevertheless laid a chastening hand upon his fellow citizens. In an ironic vein that was perhaps his best medium he would hint at the community's lack of culture, though he would be the first to defend the city from such assaults from without the walls. He prepared the way for the coming of Edmund Clarence Stedman with announcements of a series of bizarre entertainments in the poet's honor, including a street parade in which the meat-packing industry was to be elaborately represented. He gave circulation to a story, purely fanciful, that Joel Chandler Harris was born in Africa, where his parents were missionaries, thus accounting for "Uncle Remus's" intimate acquaintance with negro characters and folklore. His devotion to journalism was such that he preferred to publish his verses in his newspaper rather than in magazines, often hoarding them for weeks that he might fill a column with poems and create the impression that they were all flung off as part of the day's work, though, as a matter of fact, they were the result of the most painstaking labor. With his legs thrown across a table he wrote, on a pad held in his lap, the minute, perpendicular hand, with its monkish rubrications, that gave distinction to all his "copy." Among other accomplishments he was a capital recitationist and mimic. There was no end to the variety of ways in which he could interest and amuse a company. He was so pre-eminently a social being that it was difficult to understand how he produced so much when he yielded so readily to any suggestion to strike work for any enterprise that promised diversion. I linger upon his name not because of his talents merely but because he was in a very true sense the protagonist of the city in those years; a veritable *genius loci* who expressed a Chicago, "wilful, young," that was disposed to stick its tongue in its cheek in the presence of the most exalted gods.

My Chicago of the consulship of Plancus was illuminated also by the National League ball club, whose roster contained "names to fill a Roman line"—"Pop" Anson, Clarkson, Williamson, Ryan, Pfeffer, and "Mike" Kelley. Chicago displayed hatchments of woe on her portals when Kelley was "sold to Boston" for $10,000! In his biography of Field Mr. Slason Thompson has preserved this characteristic paragraph—only one of many in which the wit, humorist, and poet paid tribute to Kelley's genius:

"Benjamin Harrison is a good, honest, patriotic man, and we like him. But he never stole second base in all his life and he could not swat Mickey Welch's down curves over the left-field fence. Therefore, we say again, as we have said many times before, that, much as we revere Benjamin Harrison's purity and amiability, we cannot but accord the tribute of our sincerest admiration to that paragon of American manhood, Michael J. Kelley."

III

It must be said for Chicago that to the best of her ability her iniquities are kept in the open; she conceals nothing; it is all there for your observation if you are disposed to pry into the heart of the matter. The rectilinear system of streets exposes the whole city to the sun's eye. One is struck by the great number of foreign faces, and by faces that show a blending of races—a step, perhaps, toward the evolution of some new American type. On Michigan Avenue, where on fair afternoons something of the brilliant spectacle of Fifth Avenue is reproduced, women in bright turbans, men in modifications of their national garb—Syrians, Greeks, Turks, Russians and what-not—are caught up and hurried along in the crowd. In the shopping centres of Wabash Avenue and State Street the foreign element is present constantly, and even since the war's abatement of immigration these potential citizens are daily in evidence in the railway-stations. Yet one has nowhere the sense of congestion that is so depressing in New York's East Side; the overcrowding is not so apparent even where the conditions are the worst Chicago has to offer.

My search for the picturesque had been disappointing until, quite undirected, I stumbled into Maxwell Street one winter morning and found its Jewish market to my liking. The "Ham Fair" in Paris is richer in antiquarian loot, but Maxwell Street is enough; 'twill serve! Here we have squalor, perhaps, and yet a pretty clean and a wholly orderly squalor. Innumerable booths litter the sidewalks of this thoroughfare between Halstead and Jefferson Streets, and merchandise and customers overflow into the streets until traffic is blocked. Fruits, vegetables, meats, fowls, raiment of every kind are offered. Bushel-baskets are the ordained receptacle for men's hats. A fine leisure characterizes the movements and informs the methods of the cautious purchaser. Cages of pigeons proudly surmounting coops of fowls suggested that their elevation might be attributable to some special sanctity or reservation for sacrificial rites. A cynical policeman (I saw but one guardian of the peace in the course of three visits) rudely dispelled this illusion with a hint that these birds, enjoying a free range of the air, had doubtless been feloniously captured for exposure to sale in the market-place—an imputation upon the bearded keepers of the bird bazaars that I reject with scorn. Negroes occasionally cross the bounds of their own quarter to shop among these children of the Ghettos—I wonder whether by some instinctive confidence in the good-will of a people who like themselves do daily battle with the most deeply planted of all prejudices.

**The "Ham Fair" in Paris is richer in antiquarian loot,
but Maxwell Street is enough; 'twill serve!**

Chicago is rich in types; human nature is comprehensively represented with its best and worst. It should be possible to find here, midway of the seas, the typical American, but I am mistrustful of my powers of selection in so grave a matter. There are too many men observable in office-buildings and in clubs who might pass as typical New Yorkers if they were encountered in Fifth Avenue, to make possible any safe choice for the artist's pencil. There is no denying that the average Chicagoan is less "smart" than the New Yorker. The pressing of clothes and nice differentiations in haberdashery seem to be less important to the male here than to his New York cousin. I spent an anxious Sunday morning in quest of the silk hat, and reviewed the departing worshippers in the neighborhood of many temples in this search, but the only toppers I found were the crowning embellishments of two colored gentlemen in South State Street.

Perhaps the typical Chicagoan is the commuter who, after the day's hurry and fret, ponders the city's needs calmly by the lake shore or in prairie villages. Chicago's suburbs are felicitously named—Kenilworth, Winnetka, Hubbard Woods, Ravinia, Wilmette, Oak Park, and Lake Forest. But neither the opulence of Lake Forest and Winnetka, nor polo and a famous golf-course at Wheaton can obscure the merits of Evanston. The urban Chicagoan becomes violent at the mention of Evanston, yet here we find a reservoir of the true Western folksiness, and Chicago profits by its propinquity. Evanston goes to church, Evanston reads, Evanston is shamelessly high-brow with a firm substratum of evangelicanism. Here, on spring mornings, Chopin floats through many windows across the pleasantest of hedges and Dostoyefsky is enthroned by the evening lamp. The girl who is always at the tennis-nets or on the golf-links of Evanston is the same girl one has heard at the piano, or whose profile is limned against the lamp with the green shade as she ponders the Russians. She is symbolic and evocative of Chicago *in altissimo*. Her father climbs the heights perforce that he may not be deprived of her society. Fitted by nature to adorn the bright halls of romance, she is the sternest of realists. She discusses politics with sophistication, and you may be sure she belongs to many societies and can wield the gavel with grace and ease. She buries herself at times in a city settlement, for nothing is so important to this young woman as the uplift of the race; and in so far as the race's destiny is in her hands I cheerfully volunteer the opinion that its future is bright.

I hope, however, to be acquitted of ungraciousness if I say that the most delightful person I ever met in Chicago, where an exacting social taste may find amplest satisfaction, and where, in the academic shades of three universities (Northwestern, Lake Forest, and Chicago), one may find the answer to a question in any of the arts or sciences—the most refreshing and the most instructive of my encounters was with a lady who followed the vocation of a pickpocket and shoplifter. A friend of mine who is engaged in the detection of crime in another part of the universe had undertaken to introduce me to the presence of a "gunman," a species of malefactor that had previously eluded me. Meeting this detective quite unexpectedly in Chicago, he made it possible for me to observe numbers of gangsters, or persons he vouched for as such—gentlemen willing to commit murder for a fee so ridiculously low that it would be immoral for me to name it.

It is enough that I beheld and even conversed with a worthy descendant of the murderers of Elizabethan tragedy—one who might confess, with the Second Murderer in Macbeth:

"I am one, my liege,

Whom the vile blows and buffets of the world

Have so incens'd that I am reckless what

I do to spite the world."

But it was even more thrilling to be admitted, after a prearranged knock at the back door, into the home of a woman of years whose life has been one long battle with the social order. Assured by my friend that I was a trustworthy person, or, in the vernacular, "all right," she entered with the utmost spirit into the discussion of larceny as she had practised it. Only a week earlier she had been released from the Bridewell after serving a sentence for shoplifting, and yet her incarceration—only one of a series of imprisonments—had neither embittered her nor dampened her zest for life. She met my inquiries as to the hazards of the game with the most engaging candor. I am ashamed to confess that as she described her adventures I could understand something of the lawless joy she found in the pitting of her wits against the law. She had lived in Chicago all her life and knew its every corner. The underworld was an open book to her; she patiently translated for my benefit the thieves' argot she employed fluently. She instructed me with gusto and humor in the most approved methods of shoplifting, with warnings as to the machinery by which the big department stores protect themselves from her kind. She was equally wise as to the filching of purses, explaining that this is best done by three conspirators if a crowded street-car be the chosen scene of operations. Her own function was usually the gentle seizure of the purse, to be passed quickly back to a confederate, and he in turn was charged with the responsibility of conveying it to a third person, who was expected to drop from the rear platform and escape. Having elucidated this delicate transaction, she laughed gleefully. "Once on a Wabash Avenue car I nipped a purse from a woman's lap and passed it back, thinking a girl who was working with me was right there, but say—I handed it to a captain of police!" Her husband, a burglar of inferior talents, sitting listlessly in the dingy room that shook under the passing elevated trains, took a sniff of cocaine. When I professed interest in the proceeding she said she preferred the hypodermic, and thereupon mixed a potion for herself and thrust the needle into an arm much swollen from frequent injections. Only the other day, a year after this visit, I learned that she was again in durance, this time for an ingenious attempt to defraud an insurance company.

IV

In the field of social effort Chicago has long stood at the fore, and the experiments have continued until a good many debatable points as to method have been determined. Hull House and Miss Jane Addams are a part of American history. There are those in Chicago who are skeptical as to the value of much of the machinery employed in social betterment, but they may be silenced effectively by a question as to just what the plight of the two and a half million would be if so many high-minded people had not consecrated themselves to the task of translating America into terms of service for the guidance and encouragement of the poor and ignorant. The spirit of this endeavor is that expressed in Arnold's lines on Goethe:

"He took the suffering human race,

He read each wound, each weakness clear;

And struck his finger on the place

And said: Thou ailest here and here!"

And when the diagnosis has been made some one in this city of hope is ready with a remedy.

When I remarked to a Chicago alderman upon the great number of agencies at work in Chicago for social betterment, he said, with manifest pride: "This town is full of idealists!" What strikes the visitor is that so many of these idealists are practical-minded men and women who devote a prodigious amount of time, energy, and money to the promotion of social welfare. It is impossible to examine a cross-section anywhere without finding vestigia of welfare effort, or traces of the movements for political reform represented in the Municipal Voters' League, the Legislative League, or the City Club.

It is admitted (grudgingly in some quarters) that the strengthening of the social fabric has carried with it an appreciable elevation of political ideals, though the proof of this is less impressive than we should like to have it. It is unfortunately true that an individual may be subjected to all possible saving influences—transformed into a clean, reputable being, yet continue to view his political obligations as through a glass darkly. Nor is the average citizen of old American stock, who is satisfied, very often, to accept any kind of local government so long as he is not personally annoyed about it, a wholly inspiring example to the foreign-born. The reformer finds it necessary to work coincidentally at both ends of the social scale. The preservation of race groups in Chicago's big wards (the vote in these political units ranges from eight to thirty-six thousand), is essential to safe manipulation. The bosses are not interested in the successful operation of the melting-pot. It is much easier for them to buy votes collectively from a padrone than to negotiate with individuals whose minds have been "corrupted" by the teachers of political honesty in settlements and neighborhood houses. However, the Chicago bosses enjoy little tranquillity; some agency is constantly on their heels with an impudent investigation that endangers their best-laid devices for "protection."

As an Americanizing influence, important as a means of breaking-up race affiliations that facilitate the "delivery" of votes, Chicago has developed a type of recreation park that gives promise of the best results. The first of these were opened in the South Park district in 1905. There are now thirty-five such centres, which, without paralleling or infringing upon the work of other social agencies, greatly widen the scope of the city's social service. These parks comprise a playground with baseball diamond, tennis-courts, an outdoor swimming-pool, playgrounds for young children, and a field-house containing a large assembly-hall, club-rooms, a branch library, and shower-baths with locker-rooms for men and women. Skating is offered as a winter diversion, and the halls may be used for dances, dramatic, musical, and other neighborhood entertainments. Clubs organized for the study of civic questions meet in these houses; there are special classes for the instruction of foreigners in the mystery of citizenship; and schemes of welfare work are discussed in the neighborhood councils that are encouraged to debate municipal problems and to initiate new methods of social service. A typical centre is Dvorák Park, ninety-five per cent of whose patrons are Bohemians. Among its organizations are a Bohemian Old Settlers' Club and a Servant Girls' Chorus. Colonel H. C. Carbaugh, of the Civil Service Board of South Park Commissioners, in an instructive volume, "Human Welfare Work in Chicago," calls these park centres "public community clearing-houses." They appeal the more strongly to the neighborhoods they serve from the fact that they are provided by the municipality, and, while under careful and sympathetic supervision, are in a very true sense the property of the people. Visits are exchanged by the musical, gymnastic, or other societies of the several communities, with a view to promoting fellowship between widely separated neighborhoods.

One has but to ask in Chicago whether some particular philanthropic or welfare work has been undertaken to be borne away at once to observe that very thing in successful operation. It is a fair statement that no one need walk the streets of the city hungry. Many doors stand ajar for the despairing. A common indictment of the churches, that they have neglected the practical application of Christianity to humanity's needs, hardly holds against Chicago's churches. The Protestant Episcopal Church has long been zealous in philanthropic and welfare work, and Methodists, Presbyterians and Baptists are conspicuously active in these fields. The Catholic Church in Chicago extends a helping hand through forty-five alert and well-managed agencies. The total disbursement of the Associated Jewish Charities for the year ending May, 1916, was $593,466, and the Jewish people of Chicago contribute generously to social-welfare efforts outside their fold. The Young Men's Christian Association conducts a great number of enterprises, including a nineteen-story hotel, built at a cost of $1,350,000, which affords temporary homes to the thousands of young men who every year seek employment in Chicago. This huge structure contains 1,821 well-ventilated rooms that are rented at from thirty to fifty cents a day. The Chicago Association has twenty-nine widely distributed branches, offering recreation, vocational instruction, and spiritual guidance. The Salvation Army addresses itself tirelessly to Chicago's human problem. Colonel Carbaugh thus summarizes the army's work for the year ending in September, 1916: "At the various institutions for poor men and women 151,501 beds and meals were worked for; besides which $38,779.98 in cash was paid to the inmates for work done. To persons who were not in a position to work, or whom it was impossible to supply with work, 111,354 beds and meals, 11,330 garments and pairs of shoes, and 123 tons of coal were given without charge."

The jaunty inquirer for historical evidences—hoary ruins "out of fashion, like a rusty mail in monumental mockery"—is silenced by the multiplicity of sentry-houses that mark the line of social regeneration and security. Chicago is carving her destiny and in no small degree moulding the future of America by these laborious processes brought to bear upon humanity itself. Perhaps the seeker in quest of the spirit of Chicago better serves himself by sitting for an hour in a community centre, in a field-house, in the juvenile court, in one of the hundreds of places where the human problem is met and dealt with hourly than in perusing tables of statistics.

At every turn one is aware that no need, no abuse is neglected, and an immeasurable patience characterizes all this labor. One looks at Chicago's worst slum with a sense that after all it is not so bad, or that at any rate it is not hopeless. Nothing is hopeless in a city where the highest reach down so constantly to the lowest, where the will to protect, to save, to lift is everywhere so manifest. This will, this determination is well calculated to communicate a certain awe to the investigator: no other expression of the invincible Chicago spirit is so impressive as this.

V

Anno Urbis Conditæ may not be appended to any year in the chronicles of a city that has so repeatedly rebuilt itself and that goes cheerfully on demolishing yesterday's structures to make way for the nobler achievements of to-morrow. While the immediate effect of the World's Columbian Exposition of 1892-3 was to quicken the civic impulse and arouse Chicago to a sense of her own powers, a lasting and concrete result is found in the ambition inspired by the architectural glories of the fair to invoke the same arts for the city's permanent beautification. The genius of Mr. Daniel H. Burnham, who waved the magic wand that summoned "pillared arch and sculptured dome" out of flat prairie and established "the White City" to live as a happy memory for many millions in all lands, was enlisted for the greater task. Without the fair as a background the fine talents of Mr. Burnham and his collaborator, Mr. Edward H. Bennett, might never have been exercised upon the city. Chicago thinks in large terms, and being properly pleased with the demonstration of its ability to carry through an undertaking of heroic magnitude it immediately sought other fields to conquer. The fair had hardly closed its doors before Mr. Burnham and Mr. Bennett were engaged by the Commercial Club to prepare comprehensive plans for the perpetuation of something of the charm and beauty of the fairy city as a permanent and predominating feature of Chicago. Clearly what served so well as a temporary matter might fill the needs of all time. The architects boldly attacked the problem of establishing as the outer line, the façade of the city, something distinctive, a combination of landscape and architecture such as no other American city has ever created out of sheer pride, determination, and sound taste. Like the æsthetic problems, the practical difficulties imposed by topography, commercial pre-emptions, and legal embarrassments were intrusted only to competent and sympathetic hands. The whole plan, elaborated in a handsome volume published in 1909, with the effects contemplated happily anticipated in the colored drawings of Mr. Jules Guérin, fixed definitely an ideal and a goal.

This programme was much described and discussed at the time of its inception, and I had ignorantly assumed that it had been neglected in the pressure of matters better calculated to resound in bank clearings, but I had grossly misjudged the firmness of the Chicago fibre. The death of Mr. Burnham left the architectural responsibilities of the work in the very capable hands of Mr. Bennett. The Commercial Club, an organization of highest intelligence and influence, steadfastly supported the plan until it was reinforced by a strong public demand for its fulfilment. The movement has been greatly assisted by Mr. Charles H. Wacker, president of the plan commission and the author of a primer on the subject that is used in the public schools. Mr. Wacker's vigorous propaganda, through the press and by means of illustrated lectures in school and neighborhood houses, has tended to the democratizing of what might have passed as a fanciful scheme of no interest to the great body of the people.

With singular perversity nature vouchsafed the fewest possible aids to the architect for the embellishment of a city that had grown to prodigious size before it became conscious of its artistic deficiencies. The lake washes a flat beach, unbroken by any islanded bay to rest the eye, and the back door is level with limitless prairie. There is no hill on which to plant an acropolis, and the Chicago River (transformed into a canal by clever engineering) offered little to the landscape-architect at any stage of its history. However, the distribution of parks is excellent, and they are among the handsomest in the world. These, looped together by more than eighty miles of splendid boulevards, afford four thousand acres of open space. The early pre-emption of the lake front by railroad-tracks added to the embarrassments of the artist, but the plan devised by Messrs. Burnham and Bennett conceals them by a broadening of Grant Park that cannot fail to produce an effect of distinction and charm. Chicago has a playful habit of driving the lake back at will, and it is destined to farther recessions. When the prodigious labors involved in the plan are completed the lake may be contemplated across green esplanades, broken by lagoons; peristyles and statuary will be a feature of the transformed landscape. The new Field Museum is architecturally consonant with the general plan; a new art museum and other buildings are promised that will add to the variety and picturesqueness of the whole. With Michigan Avenue widened and brought into harmony with Grant Park, thus extended and beautified and carried across the river northward to a point defined at present by the old water-tower (one of Chicago's few antiquities), landscape architecture will have set a new mark in America. The congestion of north and south bound traffic on Michigan Avenue will be relieved by a double-decked bridge, making possible the classification of traffic and the exclusion of heavy vehicles from the main thoroughfare. All this is promised very soon, now that necessary legislation and legal decisions are clearing the way. The establishment of a civic centre, with a grouping of public buildings that would make possible further combinations in keeping with those that are to lure the eye at the lakeside is projected, but may be left for another generation to accomplish.

Chicago's absorption in social service and well-planned devices for taking away the reproach of its ugliness is not at the expense of the grave problems presented by its politics. Here again the inquirer is confronted by a formidable array of citizens, effectively organized, who are bent upon making Chicago a safe place for democracy. That Chicago shall be the best-governed city in America is the aspiration of great numbers of men and women, and one is struck once more not merely by the energy expended in these matters but by the thoroughness and far-sightedness of the efforts for political betterment. Illinois wields so great an influence in national affairs that strictly municipal questions suffer in Chicago as in every other American city where the necessities of partisan politics constantly obscure local issues. The politics of Chicago is bewilderingly complicated by the complexity of its governmental machinery.

It is staggering to find that the city has not one but, in effect, twenty-two distinct governing agencies, all intrusted with the taxing power! These include the city of Chicago, a board of education, a library board, the Municipal Tuberculosis Sanitarium, the county government of Cook County, the sanitary district of Chicago, and sixteen separate boards of park commissioners. The interests represented in these organizations are, of course, identical in so far as the taxpaying citizen is concerned. An exhaustive report of the Chicago Bureau of Public Efficiency published in January, 1917, reaches the conclusion that "this community is poorly served by its hodgepodge of irresponsible governing agencies, not only independent of one another but often pulling and hauling at cross-purposes. A single governing agency, in which should be centred all the local administrative and legislative functions of the community, but directly responsible to the voters, would be able to render services which existing agencies could not perform nearly so well, if at all, even if directed by officials of exceptional ability. The present system, however, instead of attracting to public employment men of exceptional ability, tends to keep them out, with the result that the places are left at the disposal of partisan-spoils political leaders."

The waste entailed by this multiplication of agencies and resulting diffusion of power and responsibility is illustrated by the number of occasions on which the citizen is called upon to register and vote. The election expenses of Chicago and Cook County for 1916 were more than two million dollars, an increase of one hundred per cent in four years. This does not, of course, take account of the great sums expended by candidates and party organizations, or the waste caused by the frequent interruptions to normal business. Chicago's calendar of election events for 1918 includes opportunities for registration in February, March, August, and October; city primaries in February; general primaries in September; a city election in April; and a general election in November.

Under the plan of unified government proposed by the Bureau of Efficiency there would be but three regular elections in each four-year period, two biennial elections for national and State officials, and one combined municipal and judicial election. A consolidation and reform of the judicial machinery of Cook County and Chicago is urged by the bureau, which complains that the five county courts and the municipal court of Chicago, whose functions are largely concurrent, cost annually two and a quarter million. There are six separate clerks' offices and a small army of deputy sheriffs and bailiffs to serve these courts, with an evident paralleling of labor. While the city and county expend nearly a million dollars annually for legal services, this is not the whole item, for the library board, the board of education, and committees of the city council may, on occasion, employ special counsel.

The policing of so large a city, whose very geographical position makes it a convenient way station for criminals of every sort, where so many races are to be dealt with, and where the existing form of municipal government keeps politics constantly to the fore, is beset with well-nigh insuperable obstacles. Last year the police department passed through a fierce storm with what seems to be a resulting improvement in conditions. An investigator of the Committee of Fifteen, a citizens' organization, declared in May, 1917, that ten per cent of the men on the police force are "inherently crooked and ought to be driven from the department." To which a police official retorted that for every crooked policeman there are 500 crooked citizens, an ill-tempered aspersion too shocking for acceptance. The *Chicago Daily News Almanac* records 114,625 arrests in 1915. Half of the total are set down as Americans; there were 9,508 negroes, 4,739 Germans, 2,144 Greeks, 7,644 Polanders, 5,577 Russians, 2,981 Italians, and 2,565 Irish. In that year there were 194 murders—35 fewer than in 1914. Comparisons in such matters are not profitable but it may be interesting to note that in 1915 there were 222 murders in New York; 244 in 1914; 265 in 1913. Over 3,000 keepers and inmates of Chicago gaming-houses were arrested in 1915. The cost of the police department is in excess of $7,000,000—an amount just about balanced by the license fee paid by the city's seven thousand saloons. Until recently the State law closing saloons on Sunday was ignored, but last year the city police department undertook to enforce it, with (to the casual eye) a considerable degree of success.

The report of the Bureau of Efficiency recommends the consolidation of the existing governing agencies into a single government headed by an executive of the city-manager type. Instead of a political mayor elected by popular vote the office would be filled by the city council for an indefinite tenure. The incumbent would be the executive officer of the council and he might be given a seat in that body without a vote. The council would be free to go outside the city if necessary in its search for a competent mayor under this council-manager plan. One has but to read the Chicago newspapers to be satisfied that some such change as here indicated is essential to the wise and economical government of the city. Battles between the mayor and the council, upheavals in one city department or another occur constantly with a serious loss of municipal dignity. With deep humility I confess my incompetence for the task of describing the present mayor of Chicago, Mr. William Hale Thompson, whose antics since he assumed office have given Chicago a vast amount of painful publicity. As a public official his manifold infelicities (I hope the term is sufficiently delicate) have at least served to strengthen the arguments in favor of the recall as a means of getting rid of an unfit office-holder.[D] Last year a general shaking up of the police department had hardly faded from the head-lines before the city's school system, a frequent storm-centre, caught the limelight. The schools are managed by a board of trustees appointed by the mayor. On a day last spring (1917) the board met and discharged the superintendent of schools (though retaining him temporarily), and, if we may believe the news columns of the Chicago *Tribune*, "Chicago's mayor was roped, thrown, and tied so rapidly that the crowd gasped, laughed, and broke into a cheer almost in one moment." I mention this episode, which was followed in a few weeks by the reinstatement of the superintendent with an increase of salary, as justifying the demand for a form of government that will perform its functions decently and in order and without constant disturbances of the public service that result only in the encouragement of incompetence.

The politicians will not relinquish so big a prize without a struggle; but one turns from the dark side of the picture to admire the many hopeful, persistent agencies that are addressing themselves to the correction of these evils. The best talents of the city are devoted to just these things. The trustees of the Bureau of Public Efficiency are Julius Rosenwald, Alfred L. Baker, Onward Bates, George G. Tunnell, Walter L. Fisher, Victor Elting, Allen B. Pond, and Frank I. Moulton, whose names are worthy of all honor as typical of

Chicago's most successful and public-spirited citizens. The City Club, with a membership of 2,400, is a wide-awake organization whose 27 civic committees, enlisting the services of 500 members, are constantly studying municipal questions, instituting inquiries, and initiating "movements" well calculated to annoy and alarm the powers that prey.

Space that I had reserved for some note of Chicago's industries, the vastness of the stock-yards, the great totals in beasts and dollars represented in the meat-packing business, the lake and railroad tonnage, and like matters, shrinks under pressure of what seem, on the whole, to be things of greater interest and significance. That the total receipts of live-stock for one year exceeded 14,000,000 with a cash value of $370,938,156 strikes me as less impressive than the fact that a few miles distant from the packing-houses exists an art institute, visited by approximately a million persons annually, and an art school that affords capable instruction to 3,000 students. Every encouragement is extended to these pupils, nor is the artist, once launched upon his career, neglected by the community. The city provides, through a Commission for the Encouragement of Local Art, for the purchase of paintings by Chicago artists. There are a variety of private organizations that extend a helping hand to the tyro, and lectures and concerts are abundantly provided. A few years ago the National Institute of Arts and Letters met for the first time in Chicago. It must have been with a certain humor that the citizens spread for the members, who came largely from the East, a royal banquet in the Sculpture Hall of the Institute, as though to present Donatello and Verrocchio as the real hosts of the occasion. It is by such manifestations that Chicago is prone to stifle the charge of philistinism.

Banquet given for the members of the National Institute of Arts and Letters.

With a noteworthy absence of self-consciousness, Chicago assimilates a great deal of music. The symphony orchestra, founded by Theodore Thomas and conducted since his death by Frederic Stock, offers a series of twenty-eight concerts a year. Eight thousand contributors made possible the building of Orchestra Hall, the organization's permanent home. Boston is not more addicted to symphonies than Chicago. Indeed, on afternoons when concerts are scheduled the agitations of the musically minded in popular refectories, the presence in Michigan Avenue of suburban young women, whom one identifies at sight as devotees of Bach and Brahms, suggest similar scenes that are a part of the life of Boston. The luxury of grand opera is offered for ten weeks every winter by artists of first distinction; and it was Chicago, we shall frequently be reminded, that called New York's attention to the merits of Mme. Galli-Curci. Literature too is much to the fore in Chicago, but I shall escape from the task of enumerating its many practitioners by pleading that only a volume would do justice to the subject. The contributors to Mr. Bert Leston Taylor's "Line o' Type" column in the *Tribune* testify daily to the prevalence of the poetic impulse within the city and of an alert, mustang, critical spirit.

With all its claims to cosmopolitanism one is nevertheless conscious that Chicago is only a prairie county-seat that is continually outgrowing its bounds, but is striving to maintain its early fundamental devotion to decency and order, and develop among its millions the respect for those things that are more excellent that is so distinguishing a trait of the Folks throughout the West. Chicago's strength is the strength of the soil that was won for civilization and democracy by a great and valorous body of pioneer freemen; and the Chicago spirit is that of the men and women who plunged into the West bearing in their hearts that "something pretty fine" (in Lincoln's phrase), which was the ideal of the founders of the republic. "The children of the light" are numerous enough to make the materialists and the philistines uncomfortable if not heartily ashamed of themselves; for it is rather necessary in Chicago to have "interests," to manifest some degree of curiosity touching the best that has been thought and done in the world, and to hold a commission to help and to serve the community and the nation, to win the highest esteem.

Every weakness and every element of strength in democracy, as we are experimenting with it, has definite and concrete presentment in Chicago. In the trying months preceding and following the declaration of war with Germany the city repeatedly asserted its intense patriotism. The predominating foreign-born population is German, yet once the die was cast these citizens were found, except in negligible instances, supporting the American cause as loyally as their neighbors of old American stock. The city's patriotic ardor was expressed repeatedly in popular demonstrations—beginning with a preparedness parade in June, 1916, in which 150,000 persons participated; in public gatherings designed to unify sentiment, not least noteworthy of these being the meeting in the stock-yards pavilion in May, of last year, when 12,000 people greeted Colonel Roosevelt. The visit of M. Viviani and Field-Marshal Joffre afforded the city another opportunity to manifest its devotion to the cause of democracy. Every responsibility entailed by America's entrance into the war was met immediately with an enthusiasm so hearty that the Chicago press was to be pardoned for indulging in ironic flings at the East, which had been gloomily apprehensive as to the attitude of the Middle West.

The flag flies no more blithely or securely anywhere in America than in the great city that lies at the northern edge of the prairies that gave Lincoln to be the savior of the nation. Those continuing experiments and that struggle for perfection that are the task of democracy have here their fullest manifestation, and the knowledge that these processes and undertakings are nobly guided must be a stimulus and an inspiration to all who have at heart the best that may be sought and won for America.

CHAPTER V
THE MIDDLE WEST IN POLITICS

The great interior region bounded east by the Alleghanies, north by the British dominions, west by the Rocky Mountains, and south by the line along which the culture of corn and cotton meets ... already has above 10,000,000 people, and will have 50,000,000 within fifty years if not prevented by any political folly or mistake. It contains more than one-third of the country owned by the United States—certainly more than 1,000,000 square miles. Once half as populous as Massachusetts already is, it would have more than 75,000,000 people. A glance at the map shows that, territorially speaking, it is the great body of the republic. The other parts are but marginal borders to it.—Lincoln: Annual Message to Congress, December, 1862.

I

IF a general participation in politics is essential to the successful maintenance of a democracy, then the people of the West certainly bear their share of the national burden. A great deal of history has been made in what Lincoln called "the great body of the republic," and the election of 1916 indicated very clearly the growing power of the West in national contests, and a manifestation of independence that is not negligible in any conjectures as to the issues and leadership of the immediate future.

A few weeks before the last general election I crossed a Middle Western State in company with one of its senators, a veteran politician, who had served his party as State chairman and as chairman of the national committee. In the smoking compartment was a former governor of an Eastern State and several others, representing both the major parties, who were bound for various points along the line where they were to speak that night. In our corner the talk was largely reminiscent of other times and bygone statesmen. Republicans and Democrats exchanged anecdotes with that zest which distinguishes the Middle Western politician, men of one party paying tribute to the character and ability of leaders of the other in a fine spirit of magnanimity. As the train stopped, from time to time, the United States senator went out upon the platform and shook hands with friends and acquaintances, or received reports from local leaders. Everybody on the train knew him; many of the men called him by his first name. He talked to the women about their children and asked about their husbands. The whole train caught the spirit of his cheer and friendliness, and yet he had been for a dozen years the most abused man in his State. This was all in the day's work, a part of what has been called the great American game. The West makes something intimate and domestic of its politics, and the idea that statesmen must "keep close to the people" is not all humbug, not at least in the sense that they hold their power very largely through their social qualities. They must, as we say, be "folks."

Apart from wars, the quadrennial presidential campaigns are America's one great national expression in terms of drama; but through months in which the average citizen goes about his business, grateful for a year free of political turmoil, the political machinery is never idle. No matter how badly defeated a party may be, its State organization must not be permitted to fall to pieces; for the perfecting of an organization demands hard work and much money. There is always a great deal of inner plotting preliminary to a State or national contest, and much of this is wholly without the knowledge of the quiet citizen whose active interests are never aroused until a campaign is well launched. In State capitals and other centres men meet, as though by chance, and in hotel-rooms debate matters of which the public hears only when differences have been reconciled and a harmonious plan of action has been adopted. Not a day passes even in an "off year" when in the corn belt men are not travelling somewhere on political errands. There are fences to repair, local conditions to analyze, and organizations to perfect against the coming of the next campaign. In a Western State I met within the year two men who had just visited their governor for the purpose of throwing some "pep" into him. They had helped to elect him and felt free to beard him in the capitol to caution him as to his conduct. It is impossible to step off a train anywhere between Pittsburgh and Denver without becoming acutely conscious that much politics is forward. One campaign "doth tread upon another's heel, so fast they follow." This does not mean merely that the leaders in party organizations meet constantly for conferences, or that candidates are plotting a long way ahead to secure nominations, but that the great body of the people—the Folks themselves—are ceaselessly discussing new movements or taking the measure of public servants.

The politician lives by admiration; he likes to be pointed out, to have men press about him to shake his hand. He will enter a State convention at just the right moment to be greeted with a cheer, of which a nonchalant or deprecatory wave of the hand is a sufficient recognition. Many small favors of which the public never dreams are granted to the influential politician, even when he is not an office-holder—favors that mean much to him, that contribute to his self-esteem. A friend who was secretary for several years of one of the national committees had a summer home by a quiet lake near an east-and-west railway-line. When, during a campaign, he was suddenly called to New York or Chicago he would wire the railway authorities to order one of the fast trains to pick him up at a lonely station, which it passed ordinarily at the highest speed. My friend derived the greatest satisfaction from this concession to his prominence and influence. Men who affect to despise politicians of the party to which they are opposed are nevertheless flattered by any attention from them, and they will admit, when there is no campaign forward, that in spite of their politics they are mighty good fellows. And they *are* good fellows; they have to be to retain their hold upon their constituents. There are exceptions to the rule that to succeed in politics one must be a good fellow, a folksy person, but they are few. Cold, crafty men who are not "good mixers" may sometimes gain a great deal of power, but in the Western provinces they make poor candidates. The Folks don't like 'em!

Outside of New York and Pennsylvania, where much the same phenomena are observable, there is no region where the cards are so tirelessly shuffled as in the Middle Western commonwealths, particularly in Ohio, Indiana, Illinois, and Kansas, which no party can pretend to carry jauntily in its pocket. Men enjoy the game because of its excitement, its potentialities of preferment, the chance that a few votes delivered in the right quarter may upset all calculations and send a lucky candidate for governor on his way to the Federal Senate or even to the White House. And in country towns where there isn't much to do outside of routine business the practice of politics is a welcome "side-line." There is a vast amount of fun to be got out of it; and one who is apt at the game may win a county office or "go" to the legislature.

To be summoned from a dull job in a small town to a conference called suddenly and mysteriously at the capital, to be invited to sit at the council-table with the leaders, greatly arouses the pride and vanity of men to whom, save for politics, nothing of importance ever happens. There are, I fancy, few American citizens who don't hug the delusion that they have political "influence." This vanity is responsible for much party regularity. To have influence a man must keep his record clear of any taint of independence, or else he must be influential enough as an independent to win the respect of both sides, and this latter class is exceedingly small. At some time in his life every citizen seeks an appointment for a friend, or finds himself interested in local or State or national legislation. It is in the mind of the contributor to a campaign fund that the party of his allegiance has thus a concrete expression of his fidelity, and if he "wants something" he has opened a channel through which to make a request with a reasonable degree of confidence that it will not be ignored. There was a time when it was safe to give to both sides impartially so that no matter who won the battle the contributor would have established an obligation; but this practice has not worked so satisfactorily since the institution of publicity for campaign assessments.

It is only immediately after an election that one hears criticisms of party management from within a party. A campaign is a great time-eater, and when a man has given six months or possibly a year of hard work to making an aggressive fighting machine of his party he is naturally grieved when it goes down in defeat. In the first few weeks following the election of 1916 Western Republicans complained bitterly of the conduct of the national campaign.

Unhappily, no amount of *a posteriori* reasoning can ever determine whether, if certain things had been handled differently, a result would have been changed. If Mr. Hughes had not visited California, or, venturing into that commonwealth, he had shaken the hand of Governor Hiram Johnson, or if he had remained quietly on his veranda at home and made no speeches, would he have been elected President? Speculations of this kind may alleviate the poignancy of defeat, but as a political situation is rarely or never repeated they are hardly profitable.

There are phases of political psychology that defy analysis. For example, in doubtful States there are shifting moods of hope and despair which are wholly unrelated to tangible events and not reconcilable with "polls" and other pre-election tests. Obscure influences and counter-currents may be responsible, but often the politicians do not attempt to account for these alternations of "feeling." When, without warning, the barometer at headquarters begins to fall, even the messengers and stenographers are affected. The gloom may last for a day or two or even for a week; then the chairman issues a statement "claiming" everything, every one takes heart of hope, and the dread spectre of defeat steals away to the committee-rooms of the opposition.

An interesting species are the oracles whose views are sought by partisans anxious for trustworthy "tips." These "medicine-men" may not be actively engaged in politics, or only hangers-on at headquarters, but they are supposed to be endowed with the gift of prophecy. I know several such seers whose views on no other subject are entitled to the slightest consideration, and yet I confess to a certain respect for their judgment as to the outcome of an election. Late in the fall of 1916, at a time when the result was most uncertain, a friend told me that he was wagering a large sum on Mr. Wilson's success. Asked to explain his confidence, he said he was acting on the advice of an obscure citizen, whom he named, who always "guessed right." This prophet's reasoning was wholly by inspiration; he had a "hunch." State and county committee-rooms are infested with elderly men who commune among themselves as to old, unhappy, far-off things and battles long ago, and wait for a chance to whisper some rumor into the ear of a person of importance. Their presence and their misinformation add little to the joy of the engrossed, harassed strategists, who spend much time dodging them, but appoint a subordinate of proved patience to listen to their stories.

To be successful a State chairman must possess a genius for organization and administration, and a capacity for quick decision and action. While he must make no mistakes himself, it is his business to correct the blunders of his lieutenants and turn to good account the errors of his adversary. He must know how and where to get money, and how to use it to the best advantage. There are always local conditions in his territory that require judicious handling, and he must deal with these personally or send just the right man to smooth them out. Harmony is the great watchword, and such schisms as that of the Sound Money Democrats in 1896, the Progressive split of 1912, and the frequent anti-organization fights that are a part of the great game leave much harsh jangling behind.

The West first kicked up its heels in a national campaign in the contest of 1840, when William Henry Harrison, a native of Virginia who had won renown as a soldier in the Ohio Valley and served as governor of the Northwest Territory, was the Whig candidate. The campaign was flavored with hard cider and keyed to the melody of "Tippecanoe and Tyler too." The log cabin, with a raccoon on the roof or with a pelt of the species nailed to the outer wall, and a cider-barrel seductively displayed in the foreground, were popular party symbols. The rollicking campaign songs of 1840 reflect not only the cheery pioneer spirit but the bitterness of the contest between Van Buren and Harrison. One of the most popular ballads was a buckeye-cabin song sung to the tune of "The Blue Bells of Scotland":

"Oh, how, tell me how does your buckeye cabin go?

Oh, how, tell me how does your buckeye cabin go?

It goes against the spoilsman, for well its builders know

It was Harrison who fought for the cabins long ago.

Oh, who fell before him in battle, tell me who?

Oh, who fell before him in battle, tell me who?

He drove the savage legions and British armies, too,

At the Rapids and the Thames and old Tippecanoe.

Oh, what, tell me what will little Martin do?

Oh, what, then, what will little Martin do?

He'll follow the footsteps of Price and Swartout, too,

While the log cabins ring again with Tippecanoe!"

The spirit of the '40's pervaded Western politics for many years after that strenuous campaign. Men who had voted for "Tippecanoe" Harrison were pointed out as citizens of unusual worth and dignity in my youth; and organizations of these veterans were still in existence and attentive to politics when Harrison's grandson was a candidate for the Presidency.

I find myself referring frequently to the continuing influence of the Civil War in the social and political life of these Western States. The "soldier vote" was long to be reckoned with, and it was not until Mr. Cleveland brought a new spirit into our politics that the war between the States began to fade as a political factor; and even then we were assured that if the Democrats succeeded they would pension Confederate soldiers and redeem the Confederate bonds. There were a good many of us in these border States who, having been born of soldier fathers, and with Whig and Republican antecedents, began to resent the continued emphasis of the war in every campaign; and I look back upon Mr. Cleveland's rise as of very great importance in that he was a messenger of new and attractive ideals of public service that appealed strongly to young men. But my political apostasy (I speak of my own case because it is in some sense typical) was attended with no diminution of reverence for that great citizen army that defended and saved the Union. The annual gatherings of the Grand Army of the Republic have grown pathetically smaller, but this organization is not a negligible expression of American democracy. The writing of these pages has been interrupted constantly by bugle-calls floating in from the street, by the cheers of crowds wishing Godspeed to our young army in its high adventure beyond the Atlantic, and at the moment, by stirring news of American valor and success in France. In my boyhood I viewed with awe and admiration the veterans of '61-'65 and my patriotism was deeply influenced by the atmosphere in which I was born, by acquaintance with my father's comrades, and quickened through my formative years by attendance at encampments of the Grand Army of the Republic and cheery "camp-fires" in the hall of George H. Thomas Post, Indianapolis, where privates and generals met for story-telling and the singing of war-songs. The honor which it was part of my education should be accorded those men will, I reflect, soon be the portion of their grandsons, the men of 1917-18, and we shall have very likely a new Grand Army of the Republic, with the difference that the descendants of men who fought under Grant and Sherman will meet at peaceful "camp-fires" with grandsons of the soldiers of Lee and Jackson, quite unconscious that this was ever other than a united nation.

There is a death-watch that occupies front seats at every political meeting.

II

The West has never lost its early admiration for oratory, whether from the hustings, the pulpit, or the lecture-platform. Many of the pioneer preachers of the Ohio valley were orators of distinguished ability, and their frequent joint debates on such subjects as predestination and baptism drew great audiences from the countryside. Both religious and political meetings were held preferably out of doors to accommodate the crowds that collected from the far-scattered farms. A strong voice, a confident manner, and matter so composed as to hold the attention of an audience which would not hesitate to disperse if it lost interest were prerequisites of the successful speaker. Western chronicles lay great stress upon the oratorical powers of both ministers and politicians. Henry Ward Beecher, who held a pastorate at

Indianapolis (1839-47), was already famed as an eloquent preacher before he moved to Brooklyn. Not long ago I heard a number of distinguished politicians discussing American oratory. Some one mentioned the addresses delivered by Beecher in England during the Civil War, and there was general agreement that one of these, the Liverpool speech, was probably the greatest of American orations—a sweeping statement, but its irresistible logic and a sense of the hostile atmosphere in which it was spoken may still be felt in the printed page.

The tradition of Lincoln's power as an orator is well fortified by the great company of contemporaries who wrote of him, as well as by the text of his speeches, which still vibrate with the nobility, the restrained strength, with which he addressed himself to mighty events. Neither before nor since his day has the West spoken to the East with anything approaching the majesty of his Cooper Union speech. It is certainly a far cry from that lofty utterance to Mr. Bryan's defiant cross-of-gold challenge of 1896.

The Westerner will listen attentively to a man he despises and has no intention of voting for, if he speaks well; but the standards are high. There is a death-watch that occupies front seats at every political meeting, composed of veterans who compare all later performances with some speech they heard Garfield or "Dan" Voorhees, Oliver P. Morton or John J. Ingalls deliver before the orator spouting on the platform was born. Nearly all the national conventions held in the West have been marked by memorable oratory. Colonel Robert G. Ingersoll's speech nominating Blaine at the Republican convention of 1876 held at Cincinnati (how faint that old battle-cry has become: "Blaine, Blaine, Blaine of Maine!") is often cited as one of the great American orations. "He swayed and moved and impelled and restrained and worked in all ways with the mass before him," says the Chicago *Times* report, "as if he possessed some key to the innermost mechanism that moves the human heart, and when he finished, his fine, frank face as calm as when he began, the overwrought thousands sank back in an exhaustion of unspeakable wonder and delight."

Even making allowance for the reporter's exuberance, this must have been a moving utterance, with its dramatic close:

"Like an armed warrior, like a plumed knight, James G. Blaine marched down the halls of the American Congress and threw his shining lance full and fair against the brazen foreheads of the defamers of his country and the maligners of his honor. For the Republican party to desert this gallant leader now is as though an army should desert their gallant general upon the field of battle.... Gentlemen of the convention, in the name of the great republic, the only republic that ever existed upon this earth; in the name of all her defenders and of all her supporters; in the name of all her soldiers dead upon the field of battle, and in the name of those who perished in the skeleton clutch of famine at Andersonville and Libby, whose sufferings he so vividly remembers, Illinois, Illinois nominates for the next President of this country that prince of parliamentarians, that leader of leaders—James G. Blaine."

In the fall of the same year Ingersoll delivered at Indianapolis an address to war veterans that is still cited for its peroration beginning: "The past rises before me like a dream."

The political barbecue, common in pioneer days, is about extinct, though a few such gatherings were reported in the older States of the Middle West in the last campaign. These functions, in the day of poor roads and few settlements, were a means of luring voters to a meeting with the promise of free food; it was only by such heroic feats of cookery as the broiling of a whole beef in a pit of coals that a crowd could be fed. The meat was likely to be either badly burnt, or raw, but the crowds were not fastidious, and swigs of whiskey made it more palatable. Those were days of plain speech and hard hitting, and on such occasions orators were expected to "cut loose" and flay the enemy unsparingly.

Speakers of the rabble-rouser type have passed out, though there are still orators who proceed to "shell the woods" and "burn the grass" in the old style in country districts where they are not in danger of being reported. This, however, is full of peril, as the farmer's credulity is not so easily played upon as in the old days before the R. F. D. box was planted at his gate. The farmer is the shrewdest, the most difficult, of auditors. He is little given to applause, but listens meditatively, and is not easily to be betrayed into demonstrations of approval. The orator's chance of scoring a hit before an audience of country folk depends on his ability to state his case with an appearance of fairness and to sustain it with arguments presented in simple, picturesque phraseology. Nothing could be less calculated to win the farmer's franchise than any attempt to "play down" to him. In old times the city candidate sometimes donned his fishing-clothes before venturing into country districts, but some of the most engaging demagogues the West has known appeared always in their finest raiment.

The Political Barbecue.

There has always been a considerable sprinkling of women at big Indiana rallies and also at State conventions, as far back as my memory runs; but women, I am advised, were rarely in evidence at political meetings in the West until Civil War times. The number who attended meetings in 1916 was notably large, even in States that have not yet granted general suffrage. They are most satisfactory auditors, quick to catch points and eagerly responsive with applause. The West has many women who speak exceedingly well, and the number is steadily growing. I have never heard heckling so cleverly parried as by a young woman who spoke on a Chicago street corner, during the sessions of the last Republican convention, to a crowd of men bent upon annoying her. She was unfailingly good-humored, and her retorts, delivered with the utmost good nature, gradually won the sympathy of her hearers.

The making of political speeches is exhausting labor, and only the possessor of great bodily vigor can make a long tour without a serious drain upon his physical and nervous energy. Mr. Bryan used to refer with delight to the manner in which Republicans he met, unable to pay him any other compliment, expressed their admiration for his magnificent constitution, which made it possible for him to speak so constantly without injury to his health. The fatiguing journeys, the enforced adjustment to the crowds of varying size in circumstances never twice alike, the handshaking and the conferences with local committees to which prominent speakers must submit make speaking-tours anything but the triumphal excursions they appear to be to the cheering audiences. The weary orator arrives at a town to find that instead of snatching an hour's rest he must yield to the importunity of a committee intrusted with the responsibility of showing him the sights of the city, with probably a few brief speeches at factories; and after a dinner, where he will very likely be called upon to say "just a few words," he must ride in a procession through the chill night before he addresses the big meeting. One of the most successful of Western campaigners is Thomas R. Marshall, of Indiana, twice Mr. Wilson's running mate on the presidential ticket. In 1908 Mr. Marshall was the Democratic candidate for governor and spoke in every county in the State, avoiding the usual partisan appeals, but preaching a political gospel of good cheer, with the result that he was elected by a plurality of 14,453, while Mr. Taft won the State's electoral vote by a plurality of 10,731. Mr. Marshall enjoys a wide reputation as a story-teller, both for the humor of his narratives and the art he brings to their recital.

A few dashes of local color assist in establishing the visiting orator on terms of good-fellowship with his audience. He will inform himself as to the number of broom-handles or refrigerators produced annually in the town, or the amount of barley and buckwheat that last year rewarded the toil of the noble husbandmen of the county. It is equally important for him to take counsel of the local chairman as to things to avoid, for there are sore spots in many districts which must be let alone or touched with a healing hand. The tyro who prepares a speech with the idea of giving it through a considerable territory finds quickly that the sooner he forgets his manuscript the better, so many are the concessions he must make to local conditions.

In the campaign of 1916 the Democrats made strenuous efforts to win the Progressive vote. Energetic county chairmen would lure as many Progressives as possible to the front seats at all meetings that they might learn of the admiration in which they were held by forward-looking Democrats— the bond of sympathy, the common ideals, that animated honest Democrats and their brothers, those patriotic citizens who, long weary of Republican indifference to the rights of freemen, had broken the ties of a lifetime to assert their independence. Democratic orators, with the Progressives in mind, frequently apostrophized Lincoln, that they might the better contrast the vigorous, healthy Republicanism of the '60's with the corrupt, odious thing the Republican party had become. This, of course, had to be done carefully, so that the Progressive would not experience twinges of homesickness for his old stamping-ground.

There is agreement among political managers as to the doubtful value of the "monster meetings" that are held in large centres. With plenty of money to spend and a thorough organization, it is always possible to "pull off" a big demonstration. Word passed to ward and precinct committeemen will collect a vast crowd for a parade adorned with fireworks. The size and enthusiasm of these crowds is never truly significant of party strength. One such crowd looks very much like another, and I am betraying no confidence in saying that its units are often drawn from the same sources. The participants in a procession rarely hear the speeches at the meeting of which they are the advertisement. When they reach the hall it is usually filled and their further function is to march down the aisles with bands and drum-corps to put the crowd in humor for the speeches. Frequently some belated phalanx will noisily intrude after the orator has been introduced, and he must smile and let it be seen that he understands perfectly that the interruption is due to the irrepressible enthusiasm of the intelligent voters of the grand old blank district that has never failed to support the principles of the grand old blank party.

The most satisfactory meetings are small ones, in country districts, where one or two hundred people of all parties gather, drawn by an honest curiosity as to the issues. Such meetings impose embarrassments upon the speaker, who must accommodate manner and matter to auditors disconcertingly close at hand, of whose reaction to his talk he is perfectly conscious. In an "all-day" meeting, held usually in groves that serve as rural social centres, the farmers remain in their automobiles drawn into line before the speakers' stand, and listen quietly to the programme arranged by the county chairman. Sometimes several orators are provided for the day; Republicans may take the morning, the Democrats the afternoon. Here, with the audience sitting as a jury, we have one of the processes of democracy reduced to its simplest terms.

The West is attracted by statesmen who are "human," who impress themselves upon the Folks by their amiability and good-fellowship. Benjamin Harrison was recognized as one of the ablest lawyers of the bar of his day, but he was never a popular hero and his defeat for re-election was attributable in large degree to his lack of those qualities that constitute what I have called "folksiness." In the campaign of 1888 General Harrison suffered much from the charge that he was an aristocrat, and attention was frequently called to the fact that he was the grandson of a President. Among other cartoons of the period there was one that represented Harrison as a pigmy standing in the shadow of his grandfather's tall hat. This was probably remembered by an Indiana politician who called at the White House repeatedly without being able to see the President. After several fruitless visits the secretary said to him one day: "The President cannot be seen." "My God!" exclaimed the enraged office-seeker, "has he grown as small as that?"

Probably no President has ever enjoyed greater personal popularity than Mr. McKinley. He would perform an act of kindness with a graciousness that doubled its value and he could refuse a favor without making an enemy. Former Governor Glynn of New York told me not long ago an incident illuminative of the qualities that endeared Mr. McKinley to his devoted followers. Soon after his inauguration a Democratic congressman from an Eastern State delivered in the House a speech filled with the bitterest abuse of the President. A little later this member's wife, not realizing that a savage attack of this sort would naturally make its author *persona non grata* at the White House, expressed a wish to take her young children to call on the President. The youngsters were insistent in their demand to make the visit and would not be denied. The offending representative confessed his embarrassment to Mr. Glynn, a Democratic colleague, who said he'd "feel out" the President. Mr. McKinley, declaring at once with the utmost good humor that he would be delighted to receive the lady and her children, named a day and met them with the greatest cordiality. He planted the baby on his desk to play, put them all at ease, and as they left distributed among them a huge bouquet of carnations that he had ordered specially from the conservatory. In this connection I am reminded of a story of Thomas B. Reed, who once asked President Harrison to appoint a certain constituent collector at Portland. The appointment went to another candidate for the office, and when one of Reed's friends twitted him about his lack of influence he remarked: "There are only two men in the whole State of Maine who hate me: one of them I landed in the penitentiary, and the other one Harrison has appointed collector of the port in my town!"

III

Statesmen of the "picturesque" school, who attracted attention by their scorn of conventions, or their raciness of speech, or for some obsession aired on every occasion, are well-nigh out of the picture. The West is not without its sensitiveness, and it has found that a sockless congressman, or one who makes himself ridiculous by advocating foolish measures, reflects upon the intelligence of his constituents or upon their sense of humor, and if there is anything the West prides itself upon it is its humor. We are seeing fewer statesmen of the type so blithely represented by Mr. Cannon, who enjoy in marked degree the affections of their constituents; who are kindly uncles to an entire district, not to be displaced, no matter what their shortcomings, without genuine grief. One is tempted far afield in pursuit of the elements of popularity, of which the West offers abundant material for analysis. "Dan" Voorhees, "the tall sycamore of the Wabash," was prominent in Indiana politics for many years, and his fine figure, his oratorical gifts, his sympathetic nature and reputation for generosity endeared him to many who had no patience with his politics. He was so effective as an advocate in criminal cases that the Indiana law giving defendants the final appeal was changed so that the State might counteract the influence of his familiar speech, adjustable to any case, which played upon the sympathy and magnanimity of the jurors. Allen G. Thurman, of Ohio, a man of higher intellectual gifts, was similarly enshrined in the hearts of his constituency. His bandanna was for years the symbol of Buckeye democracy, much as "blue jeans" expressed the rugged simplicity of the Hoosier democracy when, in 1876, the apparel of James D. Williams, unwisely ridiculed by the Republicans, contributed to his election to the governorship over General Harrison, the "kid-glove" candidate. Kansas was much in evidence in those years when it was so ably represented in the Senate by the brilliant John J. Ingalls. Ingalls's oratory was enriched by a fine scholarship and enlivened by a rare gift of humor and a biting sarcasm. Once when a Pennsylvania colleague attacked Kansas Ingalls delivered a slashing reply. "Mr. President," he said, "Pennsylvania has produced but two great men: Benjamin Franklin, of Massachusetts, and Albert Gallatin, of Switzerland." On another occasion Voorhees of the blond mane aroused Ingalls's ire and the Kansan excoriated the Hoosier in a characteristic deliverance, an incident thus neatly epitomized by Eugene F. Ware, ("Ironquill"), a Kansas poet:

"Cyclone dense,

Lurid air,

Wabash hair,

Hide on fence."

Nothing is better calculated to encourage humility in young men about to enter upon a political career than a study of the roster of Congress for years only lightly veiled in "the pathos of distance." Among United States senators from the Middle West in 1863-9 were Lyman Trumbull, Richard J. Oglesby, and Richard Yates, of Illinois; Henry S. Lane, Oliver P. Morton, and Thomas A. Hendricks, of Indiana; James Harlan and Samuel J. Kirkwood, of Iowa; Samuel C. Pomeroy and James H. Lane, of Kansas; Zachariah Chandler and Jacob M. Howard, of Michigan; Alexander Ramsey and Daniel S. Norton, of Minnesota; Benjamin F. Wade and John Sherman, of Ohio.

In the lower house sat Elihu B. Washburne, Owen Lovejoy, and William R. Morrison, of Illinois; Schuyler Colfax, George W. Julian, Daniel W. Voorhees, William S. Holman, and Godlove S. Orth, of Indiana; William B.

Allison, Josiah B. Grinnell, John A. Kasson, and James F. Wilson, of Iowa; James A. Garfield, Rutherford B. Hayes, and Robert C. Schenck, of Ohio. In the same group of States in the '80's we find David Davis, John A. Logan, Joseph E. McDonald, Benjamin Harrison, Thomas W. Ferry, Henry P. Baldwin, William Windom, Samuel J. R. McMillan, Algernon S. Paddock, Alvin Saunders, M. H. Carpenter, John J. Ingalls, and Preston B. Plumb, all senators in Congress. In this same period the Ohio delegation in the lower house included Benjamin Butterworth, A. J. Warner, Thomas Ewing, Charles Foster, Frank H. Hurd, J. Warren Keifer, and William McKinley.

How many students in the high schools and colleges of these States would recognize any considerable number of these names or have any idea of the nature of the public service these men performed? To be sure, three representatives in Congress from Ohio in the years indicated, and one senator from Indiana, reached the White House; but at least two-thirds of the others enjoyed a wide reputation, either as politicians or statesmen or as both. In the years preceding the Civil War the West certainly did not lack leadership, nor did all who rendered valuable service attain conspicuous place. For example, George W. Julian, an ardent foe of slavery, a member of Congress, and in 1852 a candidate for Vice-President on the Free Soil ticket, was a political idealist, independent and courageous, and with the ability to express his opinions tersely and effectively.

It is always hazardous to compare the statesmen of one period with those of another, and veteran observers whose judgments must be treated with respect insist that the men I have mentioned were not popularly regarded in their day as the possessors of unusual abilities. Most of these men were prominent in my youth, and in some cases were still important factors when I attained my majority, and somehow they seem to "mass" as their successors do not. The fierce passions aroused in the Middle West by the slavery issue undoubtedly brought into the political arena men who in calmer times would have remained contentedly in private life. The restriction of slavery and the preservation of the Union were concrete issues that awakened a moral fervor not since apparent in our politics. Groups of people are constantly at work in the social field, to improve municipal government, or to place State politics upon a higher plane; but these movements occasion only slight tremors in contrast with the quaking of the earth through the free-soil agitation, Civil War, and reconstruction.

The men I have mentioned were, generally speaking, poor men, and the next generation found it much more comfortable and profitable to practise law or engage in business than to enter politics. I am grieved by my inability to offer substantial proof that ideals of public service in the Western provinces are higher than they were fifty or twenty years ago. I record my opinion that they are not, and that we are less ably served in the Congress than formerly, frankly to invite criticism; for these times call for a great searching for the weaknesses of democracy and, if the best talent is not finding its way into the lawmaking, administrative, and judicial branches of our State and federal governments, an obligation rests upon every citizen to find the reason and supply the remedy.

No Westerner who is devoted to the best interests of his country will encourage the belief that there is any real hostility between East and West, or that the West is incapable of viewing social and political movements in the light of reason and experience. It stood steadfastly against the extension of slavery and for the Union through years of fiery trial, and its leaders expressed the national thought and held the lines firm against opposition, concealed and open, that was kept down only by ceaseless vigilance. Even in times of financial stress it refused to hearken to the cry of the demagogue, and Greenbackism died, just as later Populism died. More significant was the failure of Mr. Bryan to win the support of the West that was essential to his success in three campaigns. We may say that it was a narrow escape, and that the West was responsible for a serious menace and a peril not too easily averted, but Mr. Bryan precipitated a storm that was bound to break and that left the air clearer. He "threw a scare" into the country just when it needed to be aroused, and some of his admonitions have borne good fruit on soil least friendly to him.

The West likes to be "preached at," and it admires a courageous evangelist even when it declines his invitation to the mourners' bench. The West liked and still likes Mr. Roosevelt, and no other American can so instantly gain the ear of the West as he. In my pilgrimages of the past year nothing has been more surprising than the change of tone with reference to the former President among Western Republicans, who declared in 1912 and reiterated in 1916 that never, never again would they countenance him.[E]

IV

One may find in the Mississippi valley, as in the Connecticut valley or anywhere else in America, just about what one wishes to find. A New England correspondent complains with some bitterness of the political conservatism he encountered in a journey through the West; he had expected to find radicalism everywhere rampant, and was disappointed that he was unable to substantiate his preconceived impression by actual contacts with the people.

If I may delicately suggest the point without making too great a concession, the West is really quite human. It has its own "slant"—its tastes and preferences that differ in ways from those of the East, the South, or the farther West; and radicals are distributed through the corn belt in about the same proportion as elsewhere. The bread-and-butter Western Folks are pretty sensible, taken in the long run, and not at all anxious to pull down the social pillars just to make a noise. They will impiously carve them a little— yes, and occasionally stick an incongruous patch on the wall of the sanctuary of democracy; but they are never wilfully destructive. And it cannot be denied that some of their architectural and decorative efforts have improved the original design. The West has saved other sections a good deal of trouble by boldly experimenting with devices it had "thought up" amid the free airs of the plains; but the West, no more than the East, will give storage to a contrivance that has been proved worthless.

The vindictive spirit that was very marked in the Western attitude toward the railroads for many years was not a gratuitous and unfounded hatred of corporations, but had a real basis in discriminations that touched vitally the life of the farmer and the struggling towns to which he carried his products. The railroads were the only corporations the West knew before the great industrial development. A railroad represented "capital," and "capital" was therefore a thing to chastise whenever opportunity offered. It has been said in bitterness of late that the hostile legislation demanded by the West "ruined the railroads." This is not a subject for discussion here, but it can hardly be denied that the railroads invited the war that was made upon them by injustices and discriminations of which the obscure shipper had a right to complain. The antagonism to railroads inspired a great deal of radicalism aimed at capital generally, and "corporate greed," "the encroachments of capital," "the money devils of Wall Street," and "special privilege" burned fiercely in our political terminology. Our experiment with government control as a war measure has, of course, given a new twist to the whole transportation problem.

The West likes to play with novelties. It has been hospitable to such devices as the initiative, the referendum, and the recall, multiplied agencies for State supervision in many directions, and it has shown in general a confidence in automatic machinery popularly designed to correct all evils. The West probably infected the rest of the country with the fallacy that the passing of a law is a complete transaction without reference to its enforcement, and Western statute-books are littered with legislation often frivolous or ill considered. There has, however, been a marked reaction and the demand is rather for less legislation and better administration. A Western governor said to me despairingly that his State is "commissioned" to death, and that he is constantly embarrassed by the difficulty of persuading competent men to accept places on his many bipartisan regulative boards.

There is a virtue in our very size as a nation and the multiplicity of interests represented by the one hundred million that make it possible for the majority to watch, as from a huge amphitheatre, the experiments in some particular arena. A new agrarian movement that originated in North Dakota in 1915 has attained formidable proportions. The Non-Partisan League (it is really a political party) seems to have sprung full-panoplied from the Equity Society, and is a successor of the Farmers' Alliance and Populism. The despised middleman was the first object of its animosity, and it began with a comprehensive programme of State-owned elevators and flour-mills, packing-houses and cold-storage plants. The League carried North Dakota in 1916, electing a governor who immediately vetoed a bill providing for a State-owned terminal elevator because the League leaders "raised their sights" as soon as they got into the trenches. They demanded unlimited bonding-power and a complete new programme embodying a radical form of State socialism. "Class struggle," says Mr. Elmer T. Peterson, an authority on the League's history, "is the key-note of its propaganda." The student of current political tendencies will do well to keep an eye on the League, as it has gained a strong foothold in the Northwest, and the co-operative features of its platform satisfy an old craving of the farmer for State assistance in the management of his business.

The League is now thoroughly organized in the Dakotas, Minnesota, Wisconsin, Montana, Idaho, and Colorado and is actively at work in Nebraska, Kansas, Oklahoma, and Texas. Governor Burnquist of Minnesota addressed a letter to its executive secretary during the primary campaign last summer in which he said:

At the time of our entrance into the European conflict your organization condemned our government for entering the war. When it became evident that this course would result in disaster for their organization they changed their course and made an eleventh-hour claim to pure loyalty, but notwithstanding this claim the National Non-Partisan League is a party of discontent. It has drawn to it the pro-German element of our State. Its leaders have been closely connected with the lawless I. W. W. and with Red Socialists. Pacifists and peace advocates whose doctrines are of benefit to Germany are among their number.

The League's activities in obstructing conscription and other war measures have been the subject of investigation by military and civil authorities. The *Leader*, the official organ of the party, recently printed, heavily capitalized, this sentiment, "The Government of the People by the Rascals for the Rich," as the key-note of its hostility to America's participation in the war.

The West is greatly given to sober second thoughts. Hospitable to new ideas as it has proved itself to be, it will stop short of a leap in the dark. There is a point at which it becomes extremely conservative. It will run like a frightened rabbit from some change which it has encouraged. But the West has a passion for social justice, and is willing to make sacrifices to gain it. The coming of the war found this its chief concern, not under the guidance of feverish agitators but from a sense that democracy, to fulfil its destiny, must make the conditions of life happy and comfortable for the great body of the people. It is not the "pee-pul" of the demagogue who are to be reckoned with in the immediate future of Western political expression, but an intelligent, earnest citizenry, anxious to view American needs with the new vision compelled by the world struggle in the defense of democracy.

The rights and privileges of citizenship long enjoyed by women of certain Western States ceased to be a vagary of the untutored wilds when last year New York adopted a constitutional amendment granting women the ballot. The fight for a federal amendment was won in the House last winter by a narrow margin, but at this writing the matter is still pending in the Senate. Many of the old arguments against the enfranchisement of women have been pretty effectually disposed of in States that were pioneers in general suffrage. I lived for three years in Colorado without being conscious of any of those disturbances to domesticity that we used to be told would follow if women were projected into politics. I can testify that a male voter may register and cast his ballot without any feeling that the women he encounters as he performs these exalted duties have relinquished any of the ancient prerogatives of their womanhood.

There is nothing in the experience of suffrage States to justify a suspicion that women are friendlier to radical movements than men, but much to sustain the assertion that they take their politics seriously and are as intelligent in the exercise of the ballot as male voters. The old notion that the enfranchisement of women would double the vote without changing results is another fallacy; I am disposed to think them more independent than their male fellow citizens and less likely to submit meekly to party dictation.

In practically every American court- and State-house and city hall there are women holding responsible clerical positions, and, if the keeping of important records may be intrusted to women, the task of defending their exclusion from elective offices is one that I confess to be beyond my powers. Nor is there anything shocking in the presence of a woman on the floor of a legislative body. Montana sent a woman to the national Congress, and already her fellow members hear her voice without perturbation. Mrs. Agnes Riddle, a member of the Colorado Senate, is a real contributor, I shall not scruple to say, to the intelligence and wisdom of that body. Mrs. Riddle, apart from being a stateswoman, manages a dairy to its utmost details, and during the session answers the roll-call after doing a pretty full day's work on her farm. The schools of Colorado are admirably conducted by Mrs. C. C. Bradford, who has thrice been re-elected superintendent of public instruction. The deputy attorney-general of Colorado, Miss Clara Ruth Mozzor, sits at her desk as composedly as though she were not the first woman to gain this political and professional recognition in the Centennial Commonwealth. I am moved to ask whether we shall not find for the enfranchised woman who becomes active in public affairs some more felicitous and gallant term than politician—a word much soiled from long application to the corrupt male, and perhaps the Federation of Women's Clubs will assist in this matter.

V

As the saying became trite, almost before news of our entrance into the world war had reached the nation's farthest borders, that we should emerge from the conflict a new and a very different America, it becomes of interest to keep in mind the manner and the spirit in which we entered into the mighty struggle. It was not merely in the mind of people everywhere, on the 2d of April, 1917, that the nation was face to face with a contest that would tax its powers to the utmost, but that our internal affairs would be subjected to serious trial, and that parties and party policies would inevitably experience changes of greatest moment before another general election. When this is read the congressional campaign will be gathering headway; as I write, public attention is turning, rather impatiently it must be said, to the prospects of a campaign that is likely to pursue its course to the accompaniment of booming cannon overseas. How much the conduct of the war by the administration in power will figure in the pending contest is not yet apparent; but as the rapid succession of events following Mr. Wilson's second inauguration have dimmed the issues of 1916, it may be well to summarize the respective attitudes of the two major parties two years ago to establish a point of orientation.

It was the chief Republican contention that the Democratic administration had failed to preserve the national honor and security in its dealings with Mexico and Germany. As political platforms are soon forgotten, it may be of interest to reproduce this paragraph of the Republican declaration of 1916:

The present administration has destroyed our influence abroad and humiliated us in our own eyes. The Republican party believes that a firm, consistent, and courageous foreign policy, always maintained by Republican Presidents in accordance with American traditions, is the best, as it is the only true way to preserve our peace and restore us to our rightful place among the nations. We believe in the pacific settlement of international disputes and favor the establishment of a world court for that purpose.

The concluding sentence is open to the criticism that it weakens what precedes it; but the Mexican plank, after denouncing "the indefensible methods of interference employed by this administration in the internal affairs of Mexico," promises to "our citizens on and near our border, and to those in Mexico, wherever they may be found, adequate and absolute protection in their lives, liberty, and property."

General Pershing had launched his punitive expedition on Mexican soil in March, and the Democratic platform adopted at St. Louis in June justifies this move; but it goes on to add:

Intervention, implying as it does military subjugation, is revolting to the people of the United States, notwithstanding the provocation to that course has been great, and should be resorted to, if at all, only as a last resort. The stubborn resistance of the President and his advisers to every demand and suggestion to enter upon it, is creditable alike to them and to the people in whose name he speaks.

As to Germany, this paragraph of the Democratic platform might almost have been written into President Wilson's message to Congress of April 2, 1917, so clearly does it set forth the spirit in which America entered into the war:

We believe that every people has the right to choose the sovereignty under which it shall live; that the small states of the world have a right to enjoy from other nations the same respect for their sovereignty and for their territorial integrity that great and powerful nations expect and insist upon, and that the world has a right to be free from every disturbance of its peace that has its origin in aggression or disregard of the rights of peoples and nations, and we believe that the time has come when it is the duty of the United States to join with the other nations of the world in any feasible association that will effectively serve these principles, to maintain inviolate the complete security of the highway of the seas for the common and unhindered use of all nations.

The impression was very general in the East that the West was apathetic or indifferent both as to the irresponsible and hostile acts of Mexicans and the growing insolence of the Imperial German Government with reference to American rights on the seas. Any such assumption was unfair at the time, and has since been disproved by the promptness and vigor with which the West responded to the call to arms. But the West had no intention of being stampeded. A Democratic President whose intellectual processes and manner of speech were radically different from those at least of his immediate predecessors, was exercising a Lincoln-like patience in his efforts to keep the country out of war. From the time the Mexican situation became threatening one might meet anywhere in the West Republicans who thought that the honor and security of the nation were being trifled with; that the President's course was inconsistent and vacillating; and even that we should have whipped Mexico into subjection and maintained an army on her soil until a stable government had been established. These views were expressed in many parts of the West by men of influence in Republican councils, and there were Democrats who held like opinions.

The Republicans were beset by two great difficulties when the national convention met. The first of these was to win back the Progressives who had broken with the party and contributed to the defeat of Mr. Taft in 1912; the second was the definition of a concrete policy touching Germany and Mexico that would appeal to the patriotic voter, without going the length of threatening war. The standpatters were in no humor to make concessions to the Progressives, who, in another part of Chicago, were unwilling to receive the olive-branch except on their own terms. Denied the joy of Mr. Roosevelt's enlivening presence to create a high moment, the spectators were aware of his ability to add to the general gloom by his telegram suggesting Senator Lodge as a compromise candidate acceptable to the Progressives. The speculatively inclined may wonder what would have happened if in one of the dreary hours of waiting Colonel Roosevelt had walked upon the platform and addressed the convention. Again, those who have leisure for political solitaire may indulge in reflections as to whether Senator Lodge would not have appealed to the West quite as strongly as Mr. Hughes. The West, presumably, was not interested in Senator Lodge, though I timidly suggest that if a New Jersey candidate can be elected and re-elected with the aid of the West, Massachusetts need not so modestly hang in the background when a national convention orders the roll-call of the States for favorite sons.

There was little question at any time from the hour the convention opened that Mr. Hughes would be the nominee, and I believe it is a fair statement that he was the candidate the Democrats feared most. The country had formed a good opinion of him as a man of independence and courage, and, having strictly observed the silence enjoined by his position on the bench during the Republican family quarrel of four years earlier, he was looked upon as a candidate well fitted to rally the Progressives and lead a united party to victory.

The West waited and listened. While it had seemed a "safe play" for the Republicans to attack the Democratic administration for its course with Mexico and Germany, the presentation of the case to the people was attended with serious embarrassments. The obvious alternative of Mr. Wilson's policy was war. The West was not at all anxious for war; it certainly did not want two wars. If war could be averted by negotiation the West was in a mood to be satisfied with that solution. Republican campaigners were aware of the danger of arraigning the administration for not going to war and contented themselves with attacks upon what they declared to be a shifty and wobbly policy. The West's sense of fair play was, I think, roused by the vast amount of destructive criticism launched against the administration unaccompanied by any constructive programme. The President had grown in public respect and confidence; the West had seen and heard him since he became a national figure, and he did not look or talk like a man who would out of sheer contrariness trifle with the national security and honor. It may be said with truth that the average Western Democrat was not "keen" about Mr. Wilson when he first loomed as a presidential possibility. I heard a good deal of discussion by Western Democrats of Mr. Wilson's availability in 1910-11, and he was not looked upon with favor. He was "different"; he didn't invoke the Democratic gods in the old familiar phraseology, and he was suspected of entertaining narrow views as to "spoils," such as caused so much heartache among the truly loyal in Mr. Cleveland's two administrations.

The Democratic campaign slogan, "He has kept us out of war!" was not met with the definite challenge that he should have got us into war. Jingoism was well muffled. What passed for apathy was really a deep concern as to the outcome of our pressing international difficulties, an anxiety to weigh the points at issue soberly. Western managers constantly warned visiting orators to beware of "abusing the opposition," as there were men and women of all political faiths in the audiences. Both sides were timid where the German vote was concerned, the Democrats alarmed lest the "strict accountability" attitude of the President toward the Imperial German Government would damage the party's chances, and the Republicans embarrassed by the danger of openly appealing to the hyphenates when the Republican campaign turned upon an arraignment of the President for not dealing drastically enough with German encroachment upon American rights. In view of the mighty sweep of events since the election, all this seems tame and puerile, and reminds us that there is a vast amount of punk in politics.

In the West there are no indications that an effect of the war will be to awaken new radical movements or strengthen tendencies that were apparent before America sounded the call to arms. I have dwelt upon the sobriety with which the West approached the election of 1916 merely as an emphasis of this. We shall have once more a "soldier vote" to reckon with in our politics, and the effect of their participation in the world struggle upon the young men who have crossed the sea to fight for democracy is an interesting matter for speculation. One thing certain is that the war has dealt the greatest blow ever administered to American sectionalism. We were prone for years to consider our national life in a local spirit, and the political parties expended much energy in attempts to reconcile the demands and needs of one division of the States with those of another. The prolonged debate of the tariff as a partisan issue is a noteworthy instance of this. The farmer, the industrial laborer, the capitalist have all been the objects of special consideration. One argument had to be prepared for the cotton-grower in the South; another for the New England mill-hands who spun his product; still another for the mill-owner. The farm-hand and the mechanic in the neighboring manufacturing town had to be reached by different lines of reasoning. Our statesmanship, East and West, has been of the knot-hole variety—rarely has a man risen to the top of the fence for a broad view of the whole field. What will be acceptable to the South? What does the West want? We have had this sort of thing through many years, both as to national policies and as to candidates for the presidency, and its effect has been to prevent the development of sound national policies.

The Republican party has addressed itself energetically to the business of reorganization. The national committee met at St. Louis in February to choose a new chairman in place of Mr. William R. Willcox, and the contest for this important position was not without its significance. The standpatters yielded under pressure, and after a forty-eight-hour deadlock the election of Mr. Will H. Hays, of Indiana, assured a hospitable open-door policy toward all prodigals. In 1916 Mr. Hays, as chairman of the Republican State committee, carried Indiana against heavy odds and established himself as one of the ablest political managers the West has known. As the country is likely to hear a good deal of him in the next two years, I may note that he is a man of education, high-minded, resourceful, endowed with prodigious energy and trained and tested executive ability. A lawyer in a town of five thousand people, he served his political apprenticeship in all capacities from precinct committeeman to the State chairmanship. Mr. Hays organized and was the first chairman of the Indiana State Council of Defense, and made it a thoroughly effective instrument for the co-ordination of the State's war resources and the diffusion of an ardent patriotism. Indeed the methods of the Indiana Council were so admirable that they were adopted by several other States. It is in the blood of all Hoosiers to suspect partisan motives where none exists, but it is to Mr. Hays's credit that he directed Indiana's war work, until he resigned to accept the national chairmanship, with the support and to the satisfaction of every loyal citizen without respect to party. Mr. Hays is essentially a Westerner, with the original Wabash tang; and his humor and a knack of coining memorable phrases are not the least important items of his equipment for politics. He is frank and outspoken, with no affectations of mystery, and as his methods are conciliatory and assimilative the chances are excellent for a Republican rejuvenation.

The burden of prosecuting the war to a conclusive peace that shall realize the American aims repeatedly set forth by President Wilson is upon the Democratic administration. The West awaits with the same seriousness with which it pondered the problems of 1916 the definition of new issues touching vitally our social, industrial, and financial affairs, and our relations with other nations, that will press for attention the instant the last shot is fired. In the mid-summer of 1918 only the most venturesome political prophets are predicting either the issues or the leaders of 1920. Events which it is impossible to forecast will create issues and possibly lift up new leaders not now prominent in national politics. A successful conclusion of the war before the national conventions meet two years hence would give President Wilson and his party an enormous prestige. On the other hand, if the war should be prolonged we shall witness inevitably the development of a sentiment for change based upon public anxiety to hasten the day of peace. These things are on the knees of the gods.

In both parties there is to-day a melancholy deficiency of presidential timber. It cannot be denied that Republican hopes, very generally, are centred in Mr. Roosevelt; this is clearly apparent throughout the West. In the Democratic State convention held at Indianapolis, June 18, tumultuous enthusiasm was awakened by the chairman, former Governor Samuel M. Ralston, who boldly declared for Wilson in 1920—the first utterance of the kind before any body of like representative character. However, the immediate business of the nation is to win the war, and there is evident in the West no disposition to suffer this predominating issue to be obscured by partisanship. Indeed since America took up arms nothing has been more marked in the Western States than the sinking of partisanship in a whole-hearted support of the government and a generous response to all the demands of the war. In meetings called in aid of war causes Democrats and Republicans have vied with each other in protestations of loyalty to the government. I know of no exception to the rule that every request from Washington has been met splendidly by Republican State governors. Indeed, there has been a lively rivalry among Middle Western States to exceed the prescribed quotas of dollars and men.

Already an effect of the war has been a closer knitting together of States and sections, a contemplation of wider horizons. It is inevitable that we shall be brought, East and West, North and South, to the realization of a new national consciousness that has long been the imperative need of our politics. And in all the impending changes, readjustments, and conciliations the country may look for hearty co-operation to a West grown amazingly conservative and capable of astonishing manifestations of independence.

CHAPTER VI
THE SPIRIT OF THE WEST

The wise know that foolish legislation is a rope of sand, which perishes in the twisting; that the State must follow, and not lead, the character and progress of the citizen; the strongest usurper is quickly got rid of; and they only who build on Ideas, build for eternity; and that the form of government which prevails is the expression of what cultivation exists in the population which permits it.—EMERSON.

I

MUCH water has flowed under the bridge since these papers were undertaken, and I cheerfully confess that in the course of the year I have learned a great deal about the West. My observations began at Denver when the land was still at peace, and continued through the hour of the momentous decision and the subsequent months of preparation. The West is a place of moods and its changes of spirit are sometimes puzzling. The violence has gone out of us; we went upon a war footing with a minimum amount of noise and gesticulation. Deeply preoccupied with other matters, the West was annoyed that the Kaiser should so stupidly make it necessary for the American Republic to give him a thrashing, but as the thing had to be done the West addressed itself to the job with a grim determination to do it thoroughly.

We heard, after the election of 1916, that the result was an indication of the West's indifference to the national danger; that the Middle Western people could not be interested in a war on the farther side of the Atlantic and would suffer any indignities rather than send their sons to fight in Europe. It was charged in some quarters that the West had lost its "pep"; that the fibre had softened; that the children and the grandchildren of "Lincoln's men" were insensible to the national danger; and that thoughts of a bombardment of New York or San Francisco were not disturbing to a people remote from the sea. I am moved to remark that we of the West are less disposed to encourage the idea that we are a people apart than our friends to the eastward who often seem anxious to force this attitude upon us. We like our West and may boast and strut a little, but any intimation that we are not loyal citizens of the American Republic, jealous of its honor and security and responsive to its every call upon our patriotism and generosity, arouses our indignation.

Many of us were favored in the first years of the war with letters from Eastern friends anxious to enlighten us as to America's danger and her duty with respect to the needs of the sufferers in the wake of battle. On a day when I received a communication from New York asking "whether nothing could be done in Indiana to rouse the people to the sore need of France," a committee for French relief had just closed a week's campaign with a fund of $17,000, collected over the State in small sums and contributed very largely by school children. The Millers' Belgian Relief movement, initiated in the fall of 1914 by Mr. William C. Edgar, of Minneapolis, publisher of *The Northwestern Miller*, affords a noteworthy instance of the West's response to appeals in behalf of the people in the trampled kingdom. A call was issued November 4 for 45,000 barrels of flour, but 70,000 barrels were contributed; and this cargo was augmented by substantial gifts of blankets, clothing for women and children, and condensed milk. These supplies were distributed in Belgium under Mr. Edgar's personal direction, in co-operation with Mr. Herbert C. Hoover, chairman of the Commission for the Relief of Belgium.

Many Westerners were fighting under the British and French flags, or were serving in the French ambulance service before our entrance into the war, and the opening of the officers' training-camps in 1917 found young Westerners of the best type clamoring for admission. The Western colleges and universities cannot be too strongly praised for the patriotic fervor with which they met the crisis. One president said that if necessary he would nail up the doors of his college until the war was over. The eagerness to serve is indicated in the Regular Army enlistments for the period from June to December, 1917, in which practically all of the Middle Western States doubled and tripled the quota fixed by the War Department; and any assumption that patriotism diminishes the farther we penetrate into the interior falls before the showing of Colorado, whose response to a call for 1,598 men was answered by 3,793; and Utah multiplied her quota by 5 and Montana by 7. This takes no account of men who, in the period indicated, entered training-camps, or of naval and marine enlistments, or of the National Guard or the selective draft. More completely than ever before the West is merged into the nation. The situation when war was declared is comparable to that of householders, long engrossed with their domestic affairs and heeding little the needs of the community, who are brought to the street by a common peril and confer soberly as to ways and means of meeting it.

"The West," an Eastern critic complains, "appears always to be demanding something!" The idea of the West as an Oliver Twist with a plate insistently extended pleases me and I am unable to meet it with any plausible refutation. The West has always wanted and it will continue to want and to ask for a great many things; we may only pray that it will more and more hammer upon the federal counter, not for appropriations but for things of value for the whole. "We will try anything once!" This for long was more or less the Western attitude in politics, but we seem to have escaped from it; and the war, with its enormous demands upon our resources, its revelation of national weaknesses, caused a prompt cleaning of the slate of old, unfinished business to await the outcome.

It is an element of strength in a democracy that its political and social necessities are continuing; there is no point of rest. Obstacles, differences, criticism are all a necessary part of the eternal struggle toward perfection. What was impossible yesterday is achieved to-day and may be abandoned to-morrow. Democracy, as we have thus far practised it, is a series of experiments, a quest.

II

The enormous industrial development of the Middle West was a thing undreamed of by the pioneers, whose chief concern was with the soil; there was no way of anticipating the economic changes that have been forced upon attention by the growth of cities and States. Minnesota had been a State thirteen years when in 1871 Proctor Knott, in a speech in Congress, ridiculed the then unknown name of Duluth: "The word fell upon my ear with a peculiar and indescribable charm, like the gentle murmur of a low fountain stealing forth in the midst of roses, or the soft, sweet accent of an angel's whisper in the bright, joyous dream of sleeping innocence." And yet Duluth has become indeed a zenith city of the saltless seas, and the manufactured products of Minnesota have an annual value approximating $500,000,000.

The first artisans, the blacksmiths and wagon-makers, and the women weaving cloth and fashioning the garments for their families in Ohio, Indiana, Illinois, and Missouri, never dreamed that the manufactures of these States alone would attain a value of $5,500,000,000, approximately a fifth of the nation's total. The original social and economic structure was not prepared for this mighty growth. States in which the soil was tilled almost wholly by the owners of the land were unexpectedly confronted with social and economic questions foreign to all their experience. Rural legislators were called upon to deal with questions of which they had only the most imperfect understanding. They were bewildered to find the towns nearest them, which had been only trading centres for the farmer, asking for legislation touching working hours, housing, and child labor, and for modifications of local government made necessary by growth and radical changes in social conditions. I remember my surprise to find not long ago that a small town I had known all my life had become an industrial centre where the citizens were gravely discussing their responsibilities to the laborers who had suddenly been added to the population.

The preponderating element in the original occupation of the Middle Western States was American, derived from the older States; and the precipitation into the Mississippi valley industrial centres of great bodies of foreigners, many of them only vaguely aware of the purposes and methods of democracy, added an element of confusion and peril to State and national politics. The perplexities and dangers of municipal government were multiplied in the larger cities by the injection into the electorate of the hordes from overseas that poured into States whose government and laws had been fashioned to meet the needs of a homogeneous people who lived close to the soil.

The war that has emphasized so many needs and dangers has sharply accentuated the growing power of labor. Certain manifestations of this may no longer be viewed in the light of local disturbances and agitations but with an eye upon impending world changes. Whatever the questions of social and economic reconstruction that Europe must face, they will be hardly less acutely presented in America; and these matters are being discussed in the West with a reassuring sobriety. The Industrial Workers of the World has widely advertised itself by its lawlessness, in recent years, and its obstructive tactics with respect to America's preparations for war have focussed attention upon it as an organization utterly inconsonant with American institutions. An arresting incident of recent years was the trial, in 1912, in the United States Court for the District of Indiana, of forty-two officers and members of the International Association of Structural Iron Workers for the dynamiting of buildings and bridges throughout the country. The trial lasted three months, and the disclosures, pointing to a thoroughly organized conspiracy of destruction, were of the most startling character. Thirty-eight of the defendants were convicted. The influence of labor in the great industrial States of the West is very great, and not a negligible factor in the politics of the immediate future. What industrial labor has gained has been through constant pressure of its organizations; and yet the changes of the past fifty years have been so gradual as to present, in the retrospect, the appearance of an evolution.

There is little to support an assumption that the West in these critical hours will not take counsel of reason; and it is an interesting circumstance that the West has just now no one who may be pointed to as its spokesman. No one is speaking for the West; the West has learned to think and to speak for itself. "Organized emotion" (I believe the phrase is President Lowell's) may again become a power for mischief in these plains that lend so amiable an ear to the orator; but the new seriousness of which I have attempted to give some hint in the progress of these papers, and the increasing political independence of the Western people, encourage the belief that whatever lies before us in the way of momentous change, the West will not be led or driven to ill-considered action.

In spite of many signs of a drift toward social democracy, individualism is still the dominant "note" in these Middle Western States, apart from the industrial centres where socialism has indisputably made great headway. It may be that American political and social phenomena are best observed in States whose earliest settlement is so recent as to form a background for contrast. We have still markedly in the Mississippi valley the individualistic point of view of the pioneer who thought out his problems alone and was restrained by pride from confessing his needs to his neighbors. In a region where capital has been most bitterly assaulted it has been more particularly in the pursuit of redress for local grievances. The agrarian attacks upon railroads are an instance of this. The farmer wants quick and cheap access to markets, and he favors co-operative elevators because he has felt for years that the middleman poured too many grains out of the bushel for his services. In so far as the farmer's relations with the State are concerned, he has received from the government a great many things for which, broadly speaking, he has not asked, notably in the development of a greater efficiency of method and a widening of social horizons.

III

When the New Englander, the Southeasterner, and the Pennsylvanian met in the Ohio valley they spoke a common language and were animated by common aims. Their differences were readily reconcilable; Southern sentiment caused tension in the Civil War period and was recognizable in politics through reconstruction and later, but it was possible for one to be classed as a Southern sympathizer or even to bear the opprobrious epithet of copperhead without having his fundamental Americanism questioned. Counties through this belt of States were named for American heroes and statesmen—Washington, Franklin, Jefferson, Hamilton, Marion, Clark, Perry—varied by French and Indian names that tinkle musically along lakes and rivers.

There was never any doubt in the early days that all who came were quickly assimilated into the body of the republic, and certainly there was no fear that any conceivable situation could ever cause the loyalty of the newly adopted citizen to be questioned. The soil was too young in the days of Knownothingism and the body of the population too soundly American for the West to be greatly roused by that movement. Nevertheless we have had in the West as elsewhere the political recognition of the race group—a particular consideration for the Irish vote or the German vote, and in the Northwestern States for the Scandinavian. The political "bosses" were not slow to throw their lines around the increasing race groups with a view to control and manipulation. Our political platforms frequently expressed "sympathy with the Irish people in their struggle for home rule," and it had always been considered "good politics" to recognize the Irish and the Germans in party nominations.

Following Germany's first hostile acts against American life and property, through the long months of waiting in which America hoped for a continuation of neutrality, we became conscious that the point of view held by citizens of American stock differed greatly from that of many—of, indeed, the greater number—of our citizens of German birth or ancestry. Until America became directly concerned it was perfectly explicable that they should sympathize with the people, if not with the government, of the German Empire. The *Lusitania* tragedy, defended in many cases openly by German sympathizers; the disclosure of the duplicity of the German ambassador, and revelations of the insidious activity and ingenious propaganda that had been in progress under the guise of pacifism—all condoned by great numbers of German-Americans—brought us to a realization of the fact that even unto the third and fourth generation the fatherland still exercised its spell upon those we had accepted unquestioningly as fellow citizens. And yet, viewed in the retrospect, the phenomenon is not so remarkable. More than any other people who have enjoyed free access to the "unguarded gates," of which Aldrich complained many years ago, the Germans have settled themselves in both town and country in colonies. Intermarriage has been very general among them, and their social fife has been circumscribed by ancestral tastes and preferences. As they prospered they made frequent visits to Germany, strengthening ties never wholly broken.

It was borne in upon us in the months following close upon the declaration of war against Germany, that many citizens of German birth, long enjoying the freedom and the opportunities of the Valley of Democracy, had not really been incorporated into the body of American citizenship, but were still, in varying degrees, loyal to the German autocracy. That in States we had proudly pointed to as typically American there should be open disloyalty or only a surly acceptance of the American Government's position with reference to a hostile foreign Power was profoundly disturbing. That amid the perils of war Americanism should become the issue in a political campaign, as in Wisconsin last April, brought us face to face with the problem of a more thorough assimilation of those we have welcomed from the Old World—a problem which when the urgent business of winning the war has been disposed of, we shall not neglect if we are wise. Wisconsin nobly asserted her loyalty, and it should be noted further that her response in enlistments, in loan subscriptions, in contributions to the Red Cross and other war benevolences have been commensurate with her wealth and in keeping with her honorable record as one of the sturdiest of American commonwealths. The rest of America should know that as soon as Wisconsin realized that she had a problem with reference to pro-Germanism, disguised or open, her greatly preponderating number of loyal citizens at once set to work to deal with the situation. It was met promptly and aggressively, and in the wide-spread campaign of education the University of Wisconsin took an important part. A series of pamphlets, straight-forward and unequivocal, written by members of the faculty and published by the State, set forth very clearly America's position and the menace to civilization of Germany's programme of frightfulness.

Governor Philipp, in a patriotic address at Sheboygan in May, on the seventieth anniversary of Wisconsin's admission to the Union, after reviewing the State's war preparations, evoked great applause by these utterances:

"There is a great deal said by some people about peace. Don't you permit yourselves to be led astray by men who come to you with some form of peace that they advocate that would be an everlasting disgrace to the American people. We cannot subscribe to any peace treaty, my friends, that does not include within its provisions an absolute and complete annihilation of the military autocracy that we have said to the world we are going to destroy. We have enlisted our soldiers with that understanding. We have asked our boys to go to France to do that, and if we quit short of fulfilling that contract with our own soldiers, those boys on the battlefield will have given their lives in vain."

In the present state of feeling it is impossible to weigh from available data the question of how far there was some sort of "understanding" between the government at Berlin and persons of German sympathies in the United States that when *Der Tag* dawned for the precipitation of the great scheme of world domination they would stand ready to assist by various processes of resistance and interference. For the many German-Americans who stood steadfastly for the American cause at all times it is unfortunate that much testimony points to some such arrangement. At this time it is difficult to be just about this, and it is far from my purpose to support an indictment that is an affront to the intelligence and honor of the many for the offenses of scattered groups and individuals; and yet through fifty years German organizations, a German-language press, the teaching of German in public schools fostered the German spirit, and the efforts made to preserve the solidarity of the German people lend color to the charge. It cannot be denied that systematic German propaganda, either open or in pacifist guise, was at work energetically throughout the West from the beginning of the war to arouse sentiment against American resistance to German encroachments.

Americans of German birth have been controlled very largely by leaders, often men of wealth, who directed them in their affairs great and small. This "system" took root in times when the immigrant, finding himself in a strange land and unfamiliar with its language, naturally sought counsel of his fellow countrymen who had already learned the ways of America. This form of leadership has established a curious habit of dependence, and makes against freedom of thought and action in the humble while augmenting the power of the strong. It has been a common thing for German parents to encourage in their children the idea of German superiority and Germany's destiny to rule the world. A gentleman whose parents, born in Germany, came to the Middle West fifty years ago told me recently that his father, who left Germany to escape military service, had sought to inculcate these ideas in the minds of his children from their earliest youth. The sneer at American institutions has been very common among Germans of this type. Another young man of German ancestry complained bitterly of this contemptuous attitude toward things American. There was, he said, a group of men who met constantly in a German clubhouse to belittle America and exalt the joys of the fatherland. Their attitude toward their adopted country was condensed into an oft-repeated formula: "What shall we think of a people whose language does not contain an equivalent for *Gemütlichkeit*!"

As part of the year's record I may speak from direct knowledge of a situation with which we were brought face to face in Indianapolis, a city of three hundred thousand people, in a State in which the centre of population for the United States has been fixed by the federal census for two decades. Indiana's capital, we like to believe, is a typical American city. Here the two tides of migration from the East and the Southeast met in the first settlement. A majestic shaft in the heart of the town testifies to the participation of Indiana in all the American wars from the Revolution; in no other State perhaps is political activity so vigorous as here. It would seem that if there exists anywhere a healthy American spirit it might be sought here with confidence. The phrase "He's an honest German" nowhere conveyed a deeper sense of rectitude and probity. Men of German birth or ancestry have repeatedly held responsible municipal and county offices. And yet this city affords a striking instance of the deleterious effect of the preservation of the race group. It must be said that the community's spirit toward these citizens was the friendliest in the world; that in the first years of the European War allowances were generously made for family ties that still bound many to the fatherland and for pride and prejudice of race. There had never been any question as to the thorough assimilation of the greater number into the body of American democracy until the beginning of the war in 1914.

When America joined with the Allies a silence fell upon those who had been supporting the German cause. The most outspoken of the German sympathizers yielded what in many cases was a grudging and reluctant assent to America's preparations for war. Others made no sign one way or the other. There were those who wished to quibble—who said that they were for America, of course, but that they were not for England; that England had begun the war to crush Germany; that the stories of atrocities were untrue.

As to the *Lusitania*, Americans had no business to disregard the warning of the Imperial German Government; and America "had no right" to ship munitions to Germany's enemies. Reports of disloyal speech or of active sedition on the part of well-known citizens were freely circulated.

German influence in the public schools had been marked for years, and the president of the school board was a German, active in the affairs of the National German-American Alliance. The teaching of German in the grade schools was forbidden by the Indianapolis school commissioners last year, though it is compulsory under a State law where the parents of twenty-five children request it. It was learned that "The Star-Spangled Banner" was sung in German in at least one public school as part of the instruction in the German language, and this was defended by German-Americans on the ground that knowledge of their national anthem in two languages broadened the children's appreciation of its beauties. One might wonder just how long the singing of "Die Wacht am Rhein" in a foreign language would be tolerated in Germany!

We witnessed what in many cases was a gradual and not too hearty yielding to the American position, and what in others was a refusal to discuss the matter with a protest that any question of loyalty was an insult. Suggestions that a public demonstration by German-Americans, at a time when loyalty meetings were being held by American citizens everywhere, would satisfy public clamor and protect innocent sufferers from business boycott and other manifestations of disapproval were met with indignation. The situation became acute upon the disclosure that the Independent Turnverein, a club with a handsome house that enrolled many Americans in its membership, had on New Year's Eve violated the government food regulations. The president, who had been outspoken against Germany long before America was drawn into the war, made public apology, and as a result of the flurry steps were taken immediately to change the name of the organization to the Independent Athletic Club. On Lincoln's Birthday a patriotic celebration was held in the club. On Washington's Birthday *Das Deutsche Haus*, the most important German social centre in the State, announced a change of its name to the Athenæum. In his address on this occasion Mr. Carl H. Lieber said:

With mighty resolve we have taken up arms to gain recognition for the lofty principles of a free people in unalterable opposition to autocracy and military despotism. Emerging from the mists and smoke of battle, these American principles, like brilliant handwriting in the skies, have been clearly set out by our President for the eyes of the world to see. Our country stands undivided for their realization. Impartially and unselfishly we are fighting, we feel, for justice in this world and the rights of mankind.

This from a representative citizen of the second generation satisfactorily disposed of the question of loyalty, both as to the renamed organization and the majority of its more influential members. A little later the Männerchor, another German club, changed its name to the Academy of Music.

It is only just to say that, as against many evidences of a failure to assimilate, there is gratifying testimony that a very considerable number of persons of German birth or ancestry in these States have neither encouraged nor have they been affected by attempts to diffuse and perpetuate German ideas. Many German families—I know conspicuous instances in Western cities—are in no way distinguishable from their neighbors of American stock. In one Middle Western city a German mechanic, who before coming to America served in the German army and is without any illusions as to the delights of autocracy, tells me that attachment to the fatherland is confined very largely to the more prosperous element, and that he encountered little hostility among the humbler people of German antecedents whom he attempted to convince of the justice of the American position.

The National German-American Alliance, chartered by special act of Congress in 1901, was one of the most insidious and mischievous agencies for German propaganda in America. It was a device for correlating German societies of every character—turnvereins, music societies, church organizations, and social clubs, and it is said that the Alliance had 2,500,000 members scattered through forty-seven American States. "Our own prestige," recites one of its publications, "depends upon the prestige of the fatherland, and for that reason we cannot allow any disparagement of Germany to go unpunished." It was recited in the Alliance's statement of its aims that one of its purposes was to combat "nativistic encroachments." I am assured by a German-American that this use of "nativistic" does not refer to the sense in which it was used in America in the Know-Nothing period, but that it means merely resistance to puritanical infringements upon personal freedom, with special reference to prohibition.

The compulsory teaching of German in the public schools was a frank item of the Alliance's programme. In his book, "Their True Faith and Allegiance" (1916), Mr. Gustavus Ohlinger, of Toledo, whose testimony before the Judiciary Committee of the United States Senate attracted much attention last February, describes the systematic effort to widen the sphere of the teaching of German in Western States. Ohio and Indiana have laws requiring German to be taught upon the petition of parents. Before the repeal of a similar law in Nebraska last April we find that in Nebraska City the school board had been compelled by the courts to obey the law, though less than one-third of the petitioners really intended to have their children receive instruction in German. Mr. Ohlinger thus describes the operation of the law in Omaha:

In the city of Omaha ... the State organizer of the Nebraska federation of German societies visited the schools recently and was more than pleased with what he found: the children were acquiring a typically Berlin accent, sung a number of German songs to his entire approval, and finally ended by rendering "Die Wacht am Rhein" with an enthusiasm and a gusto which could not be excelled among children of the fatherland. Four years ago Nebraska had only 90 high schools which offered instruction in German. To-day, so the Alliance reports, German is taught in 222 high schools and in the grade schools of nine cities. Omaha alone has 3,500 pupils taking German instruction. In addition to this, the State federation has been successful in obtaining an appropriation for the purchase of German books for the State circulating library. Germans have been urged to call for such books, in order to convince the State librarian that there is a popular demand and to induce further progress in this direction.

These conditions have, of course, passed, and it is for those of us who would guard jealously our rights, and honestly fulfil our obligations, as American citizens to see to it that they do not recur. The Alliance announced its voluntary dissolution some time before its charter was annulled, but the testimony before the King committee, which the government has published, will be an important source of material for the historian of the war. German propaganda and activity in the Middle West did little for the Kaiser but to make the word "German" an odious term. "German" in business titles and in club names has disappeared and German language newspapers have in many instances changed their names or gone out of business. I question whether the end of the war will witness any manifestations of magnanimity that will make possible a restoration of the teaching of German in primary and high schools.

We of the Middle West, who had thought ourselves the especial guardians of American democracy, found with dismay that the mailed fist of Berlin was clutching our public schools. In Chicago, where so much time, money, and thought are expended in the attempt to Americanize the foreign accretions, the spelling-book used in the fourth, fifth, sixth, seventh, and eighth grades consisted wholly of word-lists, with the exception of two exercises—one of ten lines, describing the aptness of the natives of Central Australia in identifying the tracks of birds and animals, and another which is here reproduced:

THE KAISER IN THE MAKING

In the *gymnasium* at Cassel the German *Kaiser* spent three years of his boyhood, a *diligent* but not a *brilliant* pupil, ranking tenth among *seventeen candidates* for the *university*.

Many tales are told of this *period* of his life, and one of them, at least, is *illuminating.*

A *professor*, it is said, wishing to curry favor with his royal pupil, informed him *overnight* of the chapter in Greek that was to be made the *subject* of the next day's lesson.

The young *prince* did what many boys would not have done. As soon as the classroom was *opened* on the following morning, he entered and wrote *conspicuously* on the blackboard the *information* that had been given him.

One may say *unhesitatingly* that a boy capable of such an action has the root of a fine *character* in him, *possesses* that *chivalrous* sense of fair play which is the nearest thing to a *religion* that may be looked for at that age, hates *meanness* and *favoritism*, and will, *wherever possible*, expose them. There is in him a *fundamental* bent toward what is clean, manly, and aboveboard.

The copy of the book before me bears the imprint, "Board of Education, City of Chicago, 1914." The Kaiser's "chivalrous sense of fair play" has, of course, ceased to be a matter of public instruction in the Western metropolis.

"Im Vaterland," a German reading-book used in a number of Western schools, states frankly in its preface that it was "made in Germany," and that "after the manuscript had been completed it was manifolded and copies were criticised by teachers in Prussia, Saxony, and Bavaria."

In contrast with the equivocal loyalty of Germans who have sought to perpetuate and accentuate the hyphen, it is a pleasure to testify to the admirable spirit with which the Jewish people in these Western States have repeatedly manifested their devotion to America. Many of these are of German birth or the children of German immigrants, and yet I am aware of no instance of a German Jew in the region most familiar to me who has not warmly supported the American cause. They have not only given generously to the Red Cross and to funds for French and Belgian relief, quite independently of their efforts in behalf of people of their own race in other countries, but they have rendered most important aid in all other branches of war activities. No finer declaration of whole-hearted Americanism has been made by any American of German birth than that expressed (significantly at Milwaukee) by Mr. Otto H. Kahn, of New York, last January:

Until the outbreak of the war, in 1914, I maintained close and active personal and business relations in Germany. I was well acquainted with a number of the leading personages of the country. I served in the German army thirty years ago. I took an active interest in furthering German art in America. I do not apologize for, nor am I ashamed of, my German birth. But I am ashamed—bitterly and grievously ashamed—of the Germany which stands convicted before the high tribunal of the world's public opinion of having planned and willed war, of the revolting deeds committed in Belgium and northern France, of the infamy of the *Lusitania* murders, of innumerable violations of The Hague conventions and the law of nations, of abominable and perfidious plotting in friendly countries, and shameless abuse of their hospitality, of crime heaped upon crime in hideous defiance of the laws of God and man.

A curious phase of this whole situation is the fact that so many thousands of Germans who found the conditions in their own empire intolerable and sought homes in America, should have fostered a sentimental attachment for the fatherland as a land of comfort and happiness, and of its ruler as a glorious Lohengrin afloat upon the river of time in a swan-boat, in an atmosphere of charm and mystery, to the accompaniment of enchanting music. In their clubs and homes they so dreamed of this Germany and talked of it in the language of the land of their illusion that the sudden transformation of their knight of the swan-boat into a war lord of frightfulness and terror, seeking to plant his iron feet upon an outraged world, has only slowly penetrated to their comprehension. It is clear that there has been on America's part a failure, that cannot be minimized or scouted, to communicate to many of the most intelligent and desirable of all our adopted citizens, the spirit of that America founded by Washington and saved by Lincoln, and all the great host who in their train—

"spread from sea to sea

A thousand leagues the zone of liberty,

And gave to man this refuge from his past,

Unkinged, unchurched, unsoldiered."

IV

In closing these papers it seems ungenerous to ignore the criticisms with which they were favored during their serial publication. To a gentleman in Colorado who insists that my definition and use of Folks and "folksiness" leave him in the dark as to my meaning, I can only suggest that a visit to certain communities which I shall be glad to choose for him, in the States of our central basin, will do much for his illumination. An intimation from another quarter that those terms as I have employed them originated in Kentucky does not distress me a particle, for are not we of Ohio, Indiana, and Illinois first cousins of the people across the Ohio? At once some one will rise to declare that all that is truly noble in the Middle West was derived from the Eastern States or from New England, and on this question I might with a good conscience write a fair brief on either side. With one Revolutionary great-grandfather, a native of Delaware, buried in Ohio, and another, a Carolinian, reposing in the soil of Kentucky, I should be content no matter where fell the judgment of the court.

To the complaint of the Chicago lady who assailed the editor for his provincialism in permitting an Easterner to abuse her city, I demur that I was born and have spent most of the years of my life within a few hours of Chicago, a city dear to me from long and rather intimate acquaintance and hallowed by most agreeable associations. The *Evening Post* of Chicago, having found the fruits of my note-book "dull" as to that metropolis, must permit me to plead that in these stirring times the significant things about a city are not its clubs, its cabarets, or its galloping "loop-hounds," but the efforts of serious-minded citizens of courage and vision to make it a better place to live in. The cynicism of those to whom the contemplation of such efforts is fatiguing, lacks novelty and is only tolerable in so far as it is a stimulus to the faithful workers in the vineyard.

I have spoken of The Valley of Democracy as being in itself a romance, and the tale as written upon hill and plain and along lake and river is well-nigh unequalled for variety and interest in the annals of mankind. I must plead that the sketchiness of these papers is due not to any lack of respect for the work of soberer chroniclers, but is attributable rather to the humility with which I have traversed a region laboriously explored by the gallant company of scholars who have established Middle Western history upon so firm a foundation. It is the view of persons whose opinions are entitled to all respect that the winning of the West is the most significant and important phase of American history. Certain it is that the story wherever one dips into it immediately quickens the heart-beat, and it is a pleasure to note the devotion and intelligence with which materials for history have been assembled in all the States embraced in my general title.

The great pioneer collector of historical material was Dr. Reuben Gold Thwaites, who made the Wisconsin Historical Society the most efficient local organization of its kind in the country. "He was the first," writes Dr. Clarence W. Alvord, of the University of Illinois, "to unite the State historical agent and the university department of history so that they give each other mutual assistance—a union which some States have brought about only lately with great difficulty, while others are still limping along on two ill-mated crutches." Dr. Thwaites was an indefatigable laborer in his chosen field, and an inspiring leader. He not only brought to light a prodigious amount of material and made it accessible to other scholars, but he communicated his enthusiasm to a noteworthy school of historians who have specialized in "sections" of the broad fertile field into which he set the first plough. Where the land is so new it is surprising and not a little amusing that there should be debatable points of history, and yet the existence of these adds zest to the labors of the younger school of historical students and writers. State historical societies have in recent years assumed a new dignity and importance, due in great measure to the fine example set by Wisconsin under Dr. Thwaites's guidance.

Frederick Jackson Turner is another historian whose interest in the West has borne fruit in works of value, and he has established new points of orientation for explorers in this field. He must always be remembered as one of the first to appreciate the significance of the Western frontier in American history, and by his writings and addresses he has done much to arouse respect for the branch in which he has specialized. Nor shall I omit Dr. John H. Finley's "The French in the Heart of America" as among recent valuable additions to historical literature. There is a charming freshness and an infectious enthusiasm in Dr. Finley's pages, attributable to his deep poetic feeling for the soil to which he was born. All writers of the history of the Northwest, of course, confess their indebtedness to Parkman, and it should not be forgotten that before Theodore Roosevelt became a distinguished figure in American public life he had written "The Winning of the West," which established a place for him among American historians.

A historical society was formed in Indiana in 1830, but as no building was ever provided for its collection, many valuable records were lost when the State capitol was torn down thirty years ago. Many documents that should have been kept within the State found their way to Wisconsin—an appropriation by the tireless Thwaites of which Indiana can hardly complain in view of the fact that she has never provided for the proper housing of historical material. Still, interest in local history, much of it having an important bearing on the national life, has never wholly died, and in recent years the *Indiana Historical Magazine* and the labors of Jacob P. Dunn, James A. Woodburn, Logan Esarey, Daniel Waite Howe, Harlow Lindley, and other students and writers have directed attention to the richness of the local field.

Illinois, slipping this year into her second century of statehood, is thoroughly awake to the significance of the Illinois country in Western development. Dr. Alvord, who, by his researches and writings, has illuminated many dark passages of Middle Western history, has taken advantage of the centenary to rouse the State to a new sense of its important share in American development. The investigator in this field is rewarded by the unearthing of treasures as satisfying as any that may fall to the hand of a Greek archæologist. The trustees of the Illinois Historical Library sent Dr. Alvord to "sherlock" an old French document reported to be in the court-house of St. Clair county. Not only was this document found but the more important Cahokia papers were discovered, bearing upon the history of the Illinois country during the British occupation and the American Revolution. Illinois has undertaken a systematic survey of county archives, which includes also a report upon manuscript material held by individuals, and the centenary is to have a fitting memorial in a five-volume State history to be produced by authoritative writers.

Iowa, jealous of her history and traditions, has a State-supported historical society with a fine list of publications to its credit. Under the direction of the society's superintendent, Dr. Benjamin F. Shambaugh, the search for material is thorough and persistent, and over forty volumes of historical material have been published. The Iowa public and college libraries are all branches of the society and depositories of its publications. The Mississippi Valley Historical Association held its eleventh annual meeting this year in St. Paul to mark the dedication of the new building erected by the State for the use of the Minnesota Historical Society.

The wide scope of Western historical inquiry is indicated in the papers of the Mississippi Valley Association, and its admirable quarterly review, in which we find monographs by the ethnologist, the specialist in exploration, and the student of political crises, such as the Lincoln-Douglas contest and the Greenback movement. Not only are the older Middle Western States producing historical matter of national importance but Montana and the Dakotas are inserting chapters that bind the Mississippi Valley to the picturesque annals of California in a continuous narrative. Minnesota, Wisconsin, Michigan, Iowa, Illinois, and Indiana have established an informal union for the prosecution of their work, one feature of which is the preparation of a "finding list" of documents in Washington. This co-ordination prevents duplication of labor and makes for unity of effort in a field of common interest.

V

I had hoped that space would permit a review in some detail of municipal government in a number of cities, but I may now emphasize only the weakness of a mere "form," or "system," where the electorate manifest too great a confidence in a device without the "follow-up" so essential to its satisfactory employment; and I shall mention Omaha, whose municipal struggle has been less advertised than that of some other Western cities. Omaha was fortunate in having numbered among its pioneers a group of men of unusual ability and foresight. First a military outpost and a trading centre for adventurous settlements, the building of the Union Pacific made it an important link between East and West, and, from being a market for agricultural products of one of the most fertile regions in the world, its interests have multiplied until it now offers a most interesting study in the interdependence and correlation of economic factors.

Like most other Western cities, Omaha grew so rapidly and was so preoccupied with business that its citizens, save for the group of the faithful who are to be found everywhere, left the matter of local government to the politicians. Bossism became intolerable, and with high hopes the people in 1912 adopted commission government; but the bosses, with their usual adaptability and resourcefulness, immediately captured the newly created offices. It is a fair consensus of local opinion that there has been little if any gain in economy or efficiency. Under the old charter city councilmen were paid $1,800; the commissioners under the new plan receive $4,500, with an extra $500 for the one chosen mayor. Several of the commissioners are equal to their responsibilities, but a citizen who is a close student of such matters says that "while in theory we were to get a much higher grade of public servants, in fact we merely elected men content to work for the lower salary and doubled and tripled their pay. We still have $1,800 men in $4,500 jobs." However, at the election last spring only one of the city commissioners was re-elected, and Omaha is hoping that the present year will show a distinct improvement in the management of its public business. Local pride is very strong in these Western cities, and from the marked anxiety to show a forward-looking spirit and a praiseworthy sensitiveness to criticism we may look confidently for a steady gain in the field of municipal government.

It is to be hoped that in the general awakening to our imperfections caused by the war, there may be a widening of these groups of patient, earnest citizens, who labor for the rationalization of municipal government. The disposition to say that "as things have been they remain" is strong upon us, but it is worth remembering that Clough also bids us "say not the struggle naught availeth." The struggle goes on courageously, and the number of those who concern themselves with the business of strengthening the national structure by pulling out the rotten timbers in our cities proceeds tirelessly.

Western cities are constantly advertising their advantages and resources, and offering free sites and other inducements to manufacturers to tempt them to move; but it occurs to me that forward-looking cities may present their advantages more alluringly by perfecting their local government and making this the burden of their appeal. We shall get nowhere with commission government or the city-manager plan until cities realize that no matter how attractive and plausible a device, it is worthless unless due consideration is given to the human equation. It is very difficult to find qualified administrators under the city-manager plan. A successful business man or even a trained engineer may fail utterly, and we seem to be at the point of creating a new profession of great opportunities for young men (and women too) in the field of municipal administration. At the University of Kansas and perhaps elsewhere courses are offered for the training of city managers. The mere teaching of municipal finance and engineering will not suffice; the courses should cover social questions and kindred matters and not neglect the psychology involved in the matter of dealing fairly and justly with the public. By giving professional dignity to positions long conferred upon the incompetent and venal we should at least destroy the cynical criticism that there are no men available for the positions created; and it is conceivable that once the idea of fitness has become implanted in a careless and indifferent public a higher standard will be set for all elective offices.

VI

No Easterner possessed of the slightest delicacy will read what follows, which is merely a memorandum for my friends and neighbors of the great Valley. We of the West have never taken kindly to criticism, chiefly because it has usually been offered in a spirit of condescension, or what in our extreme sensitiveness we have been rather eager to believe to be such. In our comfortable towns and villages we may admit weaknesses the mention of which by our cousins *in partibus infidelium* arouses our deepest ire. We shall not meekly suffer the East in its disdainful moods to play upon us with the light lash of its irony; but among ourselves we may confess that at times we have profited by Eastern criticism. After all, there is no spirit of the West that is very different from the spirit of the East. Though I only whisper it, we have, I think, rather more humor. We are friendlier, less snobbish, more sanguine in our outlook upon public matters, and have a greater confidence in democracy than the East. I have indicated with the best heart in the world certain phases and tendencies of our provinces that seem to me admirable, and others beside which I have scratched a question-mark for the contemplation of the sober-minded. I am disposed to say that the most interesting thing about us is our politics, but that, safely though we have ridden the tempest now and again, these be times when it becomes us to ponder with a new gravity the weight we carry in the national scale. Colorado, Illinois, Indiana, Iowa, Kansas, Michigan, Minnesota, Nebraska, Ohio, and Wisconsin wield 145 votes of the total of 531 in the electoral college; and in 1916 Mr. Wilson's majority was only 23. The political judgment of the nation is likely, far into the future, to be governed by the West. We dare not, if we would, carry our responsibilities lightly. We have of late been taking our politics much more seriously; a flexibility of the vote, apparent in recent contests, is highly encouraging to those of us who see a hope and a safety in the multiplication of the independents. But even with this we have done little to standardize public service; the ablest men of the West do not govern it, and the fact that this has frequently been true of the country at large can afford us no honest consolation. There is no reason why, if we are the intelligent, proud sons of democracy we imagine ourselves to be, we should not so elevate our political standards as to put other divisions of the republic to shame. There are thousands of us who at every election vote for candidates we know nothing about, or for others we would not think of intrusting with any private affair, and yet because we find their names under a certain party emblem we cheerfully turn over to such persons important public business for the honest and efficient transaction of which they have not the slightest qualification. What I am saying is merely a repetition of what has been said for years without marked effect upon the electorate. But just now, when democracy is fighting for its life in the world, we do well to give serious heed to such warnings. If we have not time or patience to perform the services required of a citizen who would be truly self-governing, then the glory of fighting for free institutions on the battle-fields of Europe is enormously diminished.

The coming of the war found the West rather hard put for any great cause upon which to expend its energy and enthusiasm. We need a good deal of enthusiasm to keep us "up to pitch," and I shall not scruple to say that, in spite of our fine showing as to every demand thus far made by the war, the roll of the drums really found us inviting the reproach passed by the prophet upon them "that lie upon beds of ivory, and stretch themselves upon their couches, and eat the lambs out of the flock, and the calves out of the midst of the stall." Over and over again, as I have travelled through the West in recent years, it has occurred to me that sorely indeed we needed an awakening. Self-satisfaction and self-contemplation are little calculated to promote that clear thinking and vigorous initiative that are essential to triumphant democracy. Yes; this may be just as true of East or South; but it is of the West that we are speaking. I shall go the length of saying that any failure of democracy "to work" here in America is more heavily chargeable upon us of these Middle Western States than upon our fellow Americans in other sections. For here we are young enough to be very conscious of all those processes by which States are formed and political and social order established. Our fathers or our grandfathers were pioneers; and from them the tradition is fresh of the toil and aspiration that went to the making of these commonwealths. We cannot deceive ourselves into believing that they did all that was necessary to perpetuate the structure, and that it is not incumbent upon us to defend, strengthen, and renew what they fashioned. We had, like many of those who have come to us from over the sea to share in our blessings, fallen into the error of assuming that America is a huge corporation in which every one participates in the dividends without reference to his part in earning them. Politically speaking, we have too great a number of those who "hang on behind" and are a dead weight upon those who bear the yoke. We must do better about this; and in no way can the West prove its fitness to wield power in the nation than through a quickening of all those forces that tend to make popular government an intelligently directed implement controlled by the fit, and not a weapon caught up and exercised ignorantly by the unfit.

Again, still speaking as one Westerner to another, our entrance into the war found us dangerously close to the point of losing something that was finely spiritual in our forebears. I am aware that an impatient shrug greets this suggestion. The spires and towers of innumerable churches decorate the Western sky-line, and I accept them for what they represent, without discussing the efficiency of the modern church or its failure or success in meeting the problems of modern life. There was apparent in the first settlers of the Mississippi valley a rugged spirituality that accounted for much in their achievements. The West was a lonesome place and religion—Catholic and Protestant—filled a need and assisted greatly in making wilderness and plain tolerable. The imagination of the pioneer was quickened and brightened by the promise of things that he believed to be eternal; the vast sweep of prairie and woodland deepened his sense of reliance upon the Infinite. This sense so happily interpreted and fittingly expressed by Lincoln is no longer discernible—at least it is not obtrusively manifest—and this seems to me a lamentable loss. Here, again, it may be said that this is not peculiar to the West; that we have only been affected by the eternal movement of the time spirit. And yet this elementary confidence in things of the spirit played an important part in the planting of the democratic ideal in the heart of America, and we can but deplore the passing of what to our immediate ancestors was so satisfying and stimulating. And here, as with other problems that I have passed with only the most superficial note, I have no solution, if indeed any be possible. I am fully conscious that I fumble for something intangible and elusive; and it may be that I am only crying vainly for the restoration of something that has gone forever. Perhaps this war came opportunely to break our precipitate rush toward materialism, and the thing we were apparently losing, the old enthusiasm for higher things, the greater leisure for self-examination and self-communion, may come again in the day of peace.

"There is always," says Woodberry, "an ideality of the human spirit" visible in all the works of democracy, and we need to be reminded of this frequently, for here in the heart of America it is of grave importance that we remain open-minded and open-hearted to that continuing idealism which must be the strength and stay of the nation.

Culture, as we commonly use the term, may properly be allowed to pass as merely another aspect of the idealism "deep in the general heart of man" that we should like to believe to be one of the great assets of the West. Still addressing the Folks, my neighbors, I will temerariously repeat an admission tucked into an earlier chapter, that here is a field where we do well to carry ourselves modestly. There was an impression common in my youth that culture of the highest order was not only possible in the West but that we Westerners were peculiarly accessible to its benignant influences and very likely to become its special guardians and apostles. Those were times when life was less complex, when the spirituality stirred by the Civil War was still very perceptible, when our enthusiasms were less insistently presented in statistics of crops and manufactures. We children of those times were encouraged to keep Emerson close at hand, for his purifying and elevating influence, and in a college town which I remember very well the professor of Greek was a venerated person and took precedence in any company over the athletic director.

In those days, that seem now so remote, it was quite respectable to speak of the humanities, and people did so without self-consciousness. But culture, the culture of the humanities, never gained that foothold in the West that had been predicted for it. That there are few signs of its permanent establishment anywhere does not conceal our failure either to implant it or to find for it any very worthy substitute. We have valiantly invested millions of dollars in education and other millions in art museums and in libraries without any resulting diffusion of what we used to be pleased to call culture. We dismiss the whole business quite characteristically by pointing with pride to handsome buildings and generous endowments in much the same spirit that we call attention to a new automobile factory. There are always the few who profit by these investments; but it is not for the few that we design them; it is for the illumination of the great mass that we spend our treasure upon them. The doctrine of the few is the old doctrine of "numbers" and "the remnant," and even at the cost of reconstructing human nature we promised to show the world that a great body of people in free American States could be made sensitive and responsive to beauty in all its forms. The humanities still struggle manfully, but without making any great headway against adverse currents. The State universities offer an infinite variety of courses in literature and the fine arts, and they are served by capable and zealous instructors, but with no resulting progress against the tide of materialism. "Culture," as a friend of mine puts it, "is on the blink." We hear reassuring reports of the State technical schools where the humanities receive a niggardly minimum of attention, and these institutions demand our heartiest admiration for the splendid work they are doing. But our development is lamentably one-sided; we have merely groups of cultivated people, just as older civilizations had them, not the great communities animated by ideals of nobility and beauty that we were promised.

In the many matters which we of the West shall be obliged to consider with reference to the nation and the rest of the world as soon as *Kultur* and its insolent presumptions have been disposed of, culture, in its ancient and honorable sense, is quite likely to make a poor fight for attention. And yet here are things, already falling into neglect, which we shall do well to scan once and yet again before parting company with them forever. There are balances as between materialism and idealism which it is desirable to maintain if the fineness and vigor of democracy and its higher inspirational values are to be further developed. Our Middle Western idealism has been expending itself in channels of social and political betterment, and it remains to be seen whether we shall be able to divert some part of its energy to the history, the literature, and the art of the past, not for cultural reasons merely but as part of our combat with provincialism and the creation of a broad and informed American spirit.

"Having in mind things true, things elevated, things just, things pure, things amiable, things of good report—having these in mind, studying and loving these, is what saves States," wrote Matthew Arnold thirty years ago. In the elaboration of a programme for the future of America that shall not ignore what is here connoted there is presented to the Middle West abundant material for new enthusiasms and endeavors, commensurate with its opportunities and obligations not merely as the Valley of Democracy but as the Valley of Decision.

THE END.

FOOTNOTES:

[A] The matter has been disposed of by the adoption of a prohibition amendment to the Federal Constitution.

[B] Kenneth Victor Elliott, of Sheridan, Indiana. He died in battle, giving his youth and his high hope of life for the America he loved with a passionate devotion.

[C] Now the Assistant Secretary of Agriculture.

[D] Mr. Thompson was re-elected April 1, 1919, by a plurality of 17,600.

[E] Colonel Roosevelt died January 6, 1919.

Milton Keynes UK
Ingram Content Group UK Ltd.
UKHW030741071024
449371UK00006B/656